Cakes & Desserts

Practical
Step-by-Step
Collection

FLAME TREE
PUBLISHING

Publisher and Creative Director: Nick Wells
Art Director: Mike Spender
Project Editor: Catherine Taylor
Editorial Planning: Rosanna Singler, Christian Anthony and Victoria Lyle
Layout Design: Mike Spender, Colin Rudderham and Vanessa Green
Digital Design and Production: Chris Herbert and Claire Walker
Proofreader: Alison Hill

Special thanks to Joseph Kelly and Connie Novis.

11 13 15 14 12

1 3 5 7 9 10 8 6 4 2

This edition first published in 2011 by
FLAME TREE PUBLISHING
Crabtree Hall, Crabtree Lane,
Fulham, London, SW6 6TY
United Kingdom

www.flametreepublishing.com

FLAME TREE is part of The Foundry Creative Media Company Limited

ISBN 978-1-84451-961-3

The CIP record for this book is available from the British Library.

Printed in China

Authors: Catherine Atkinson, Juliet Barker, Gina Steer, Vicki Smallwood,
Carol Tennant, Mari Mererid Williams, Elizabeth Wolf-Cohen and Simone Wright
Editorial (original edition): Sara Goulding and Sara Robson
Photography: Colin Bowling, Paul Forrester and Stephen Brayne
Home Economists and Stylists: Jacqueline Bellefontaine,
Mandy Phipps, Vicki Smallwood and Penny Stephens

All props supplied by Barbara Stewart at Surfaces

NOTES
All eggs are large, and all fruit and vegetables are medium, unless otherwise stated.
Recipes using uncooked eggs should be avoided by infants,
the elderly, pregnant women, and anyone suffering from a chronic illness.

Contents

Everyday Cakes

Cakes for Special Occasions

Desserts

Cleanliness in the Kitchen

It is well worth remembering that many foods can carry some form of bacteria. In most cases, the worst it will lead to is a bout of food poisoning or gastroenteritis, although for certain groups this can be more serious—the risk can be reduced or eliminated by good food hygiene and proper cooking.

Do not buy food that is past its sell-by date, and do not consume food that is past its use-by date. When buying food, use your eyes and nose. If the food looks tired, limp, or discolored, or it has a rank, acrid, or simply bad smell, do not buy or eat it under any circumstances.

Be sure to take special care when preparing raw meat and fish. A separate chopping board should be used for each; wash the knife, board, and your hands thoroughly before handling or preparing any other food.

Regularly clean, defrost, and clear out the refrigerator and freezer—it is worth checking the packaging to see exactly how long each product is safe to freeze.

Avoid handling food if suffering from an upset stomach, since bacteria can be passed through food preparation.

Dishtowels must be washed and changed regularly. Ideally, use paper towels, which can be thrown out after use. Dishtowels should be left to soak in bleach, then washed in hot water in a washing machine.

Keep the hands, cooking utensils, and food preparation surfaces clean, and do not allow pets to climb on to any work surfaces.

Buying

Avoid bulk buying where possible especially fresh produce such as meat, poultry, fish, fruit, and vegetables. Fresh foods lose their nutritional value rapidly, so buying a little at a time minimizes loss of nutrients. It also eliminates a packed refrigerator, which reduces the effectiveness of the refrigeration process.

When buying prepackaged goods such as cans or cartons of cream and yogurts, check that the packaging is intact and not damaged or pierced. Cans should not be dented, pierced, or rusty. Check the sell-by dates even for cans and packs of dry ingredients such as flour and rice. Store fresh foods in the refrigerator as soon as possible—not in the car or office.

When buying frozen foods, ensure that they are not heavily iced on the outside and the contents feel completely frozen. Make sure that the frozen foods have been stored in the cabinet at the correct storage level and the temperature is below 0°F. Pack in cool bags to transport home, and place in the freezer as soon as possible after purchase.

Preparation

Make sure that all work surfaces and utensils are clean and dry. Hygiene should be given priority at all times. Separate chopping boards should be used for raw and cooked meats, fish, and vegetables. Currently, a variety of good-quality plastic boards come in various designs and colors. This makes differentiating easier, and the plastic has the added hygienic

advantage of being washable at high temperatures in the dishwasher. If using the board for fish, first wash in cold water, then in hot to prevent odor. Also, remember that knives and utensils should always be thoroughly cleaned after use.

When cooking, be particularly careful to keep cooked and raw food separate to avoid any contamination. It is worth washing all fruits and vegetables

regardless of whether they are going to be eaten raw or lightly cooked. This rule should apply even to prewashed herbs and salads.

Do not reheat food more than once. If using a microwave, always check that the food is piping hot all the way through. (The food should reach 160°F, and needs to be cooked at that temperature for at least three minutes to ensure that all bacteria are killed.)

All poultry must be thoroughly thawed before using. Remove the food to be thawed from the freezer and place in a shallow dish to contain the juices. Leave the food in the refrigerator until it is completely thawed. A 3-lb whole chicken will take about 26–30 hours to thaw. To speed up the process, immerse the chicken in cold water. However, make sure that the water is changed regularly. When the joints can move freely and no ice crystals remain in the cavity, the bird is completely thawed.

Once thawed, remove the wrapper and pat the chicken dry. Place the

chicken in a shallow dish, cover lightly, and store as close to the base of the refrigerator as possible. The chicken should be cooked as soon as possible.

Some foods can be cooked from frozen, including many prepacked foods such as soups, sauces, casseroles, and breads. Where applicable, follow the manufacturers' directions.

Vegetables and fruits can also be cooked from frozen, but meats and fish should be thawed first. The only time food can be refrozen is when the food has been thoroughly thawed, then cooked. Once the food has cooled, then it can be frozen again. On such occasions the food can only be stored for one month.

All poultry and game (except for duck) must be cooked thoroughly. When cooked, the juices will run clear on the thickest part of the bird—the best area to try is usually the thigh. Other meats, like ground meat and pork, should be cooked all the way through. Fish should turn opaque, be firm in texture, and break easily into large flakes.

When cooking leftovers, make sure they are reheated until piping hot and

that any sauce or soup reaches boiling point first.

Storing, Refrigerating, and Freezing

Meat, poultry, fish, seafood, and dairy products should all be refrigerated. The temperature of the refrigerator should be between 34–41°F while the freezer temperature should not rise above 0°F. To ensure the optimum refrigerator and freezer

temperature, avoid leaving the door open for a long time. Try not to overstock the refrigerator, since this reduces the airflow inside and reduces the effectiveness of cooling the food within.

When refrigerating cooked food, let it cool down quickly and completely before refrigerating. Hot food will raise the temperature of the refrigerator and possibly affect or spoil other food stored inside.

Food within the refrigerator and freezer should always be covered. Raw and cooked food should be stored in separate parts of the refrigerator. Cooked food should be kept on the top shelves of the refrigerator, while raw meat, poultry, and fish should be placed on bottom shelves to avoid drips and cross-contamination. It is recommended that eggs should be refrigerated in order to maintain their freshness and shelf life.

Take care that frozen foods are not stored in the freezer for too long. Blanched vegetables can be stored for one month; beef, lamb, poultry, and pork for six months; and unblanched vegetables and fruits in syrup for a year. Oily fish and sausages should be stored for three months. Dairy products can last four to six months, while cakes and pastries should be kept in the freezer for three to six months.

High Risk Foods

Certain foods may carry risks to people who are considered vulnerable, such as the elderly, the ill, pregnant women, babies, young infants, and those with a compromised immune system.

It is advisable to avoid those foods listed below which belong to a higher-risk category.

There is a slight chance that some eggs carry the bacteria salmonella. To eliminate this risk, cook the eggs until both the yolk and the white are firm. Pay particular attention to dishes and products incorporating lightly cooked or raw eggs, which should be

eliminated from the diet. Sauces including hollandaise and mayonnaise, mousses, soufflés, and meringues all use raw or lightly cooked eggs, as do custard-based dishes, ice creams, and sorbets. These are all considered high-risk foods to the vulnerable groups mentioned above.

Certain meats and poultry also carry the potential risk of salmonella and should be cooked thoroughly until the juices run clear and there is no pinkness left. Unpasteurized products such as milk, cheese (especially soft cheese), pâté, meat (both raw and cooked) all have the potential risk of listeria.

When buying seafood, buy from a reputable source which has a high turnover, to ensure freshness. Fish should have bright, clear eyes, shiny skin, and bright pink or red gills. The fish should feel stiff to the touch, with a slight smell of sea air and iodine. The flesh of fish steaks and fillets should be translucent with no signs of discoloration. Mollusks such as scallops, clams, and mussels are sold fresh, and are still alive. Avoid any that are open or do not close when tapped lightly. In the same way, univalves should withdraw back into their shells when lightly prodded. When choosing cephalopods such as squid and octopus, they should have a firm flesh and pleasant sea smell.

As with all fish, whether it is shellfish or seafish, care is needed when freezing. It is imperative to check whether the fish has been frozen before. If it has been frozen, then it should not be frozen again under any circumstances.

Essential Ingredients

The quantities may differ, but basic baking ingredients do not vary greatly. Let us take a look at the baking ingredients that are essential.

Fat

Butter and firm block margarine are the fats most commonly used in baking. Others can also be used, such as vegetable shortening, lard, and oil. Low-fat spreads are not recommended because they break down when cooked at a high temperature. Often, it is a matter of personal preference when it comes to which fat you choose when baking, but there are a few guidelines that are important to remember.

Butter is the fat most commonly used when making cakes, especially in rich fruitcakes and the heavier sponge cakes, such as Madeira or chocolate torte; it gives a distinctive flavor to the cake. Some people favor margarine, which imparts little or no flavor to the cake. As a rule, do not use firm margarine and butter straight from the refrigerator but let it come to room temperature before using (known as "softened"). Also, it should be beaten by itself first before creaming or rubbing in. Soft margarine, sold in tubs, is a quick and easy fat that can be used straight from the refrigerator and is ideal for one-stage recipes.

Light oils, such as vegetable or sunflower, are sometimes used instead of solid fats. It is vital to follow a specific recipe because the proportions of oil to flour and eggs are different.

Fat is an integral ingredient when making pastry; again, there are a few specific guidelines to keep in mind. For a basic pastry dough, the best results are achieved by using equal amounts of lard or vegetable shortening with butter or block margarine. The amount of fat used is always half the amount of flour. Other pastries use differing amounts of ingredients. Pâte sucrée (a sweet tart pastry) uses all butter with eggs and a little sugar, while puff pastry uses a larger proportion of fat to flour and relies on the folding and rolling process as it is being made to ensure that the pastry rises and flakes well. When using a recipe, refer to the instructions to obtain the best result.

Flour

We can buy a wide range of flours, all designed for specific jobs. Bread flour, which is rich in gluten, whether it is white (shown top left of the picture here) or whole-wheat (shown top right), is best kept for bread.

Italian 00 flour is designed for making pasta and there is no substitute for this flour, but you can use all-purpose flour with good results.

Ordinary all-purpose flour is best for cakes, cookies, and sauces because it absorbs the fat easily and produces a soft, light texture. This flour comes in ordinary white, self-rising (which has the leavening agents, such as baking powder and salt, already incorporated), and whole-wheat types (whole-wheat self-rising). All-purpose flour, as the name suggests, can be used for all types of baking and sauces.

If using all-purpose flour instead of self-rising flour for cakes, cookies, or puddings, unless otherwise stated in the recipe, add $1\frac{1}{2}$ teaspoons of baking powder plus $\frac{1}{2}$ teaspoon of salt for every 1 cup of all-purpose flour. With sponge cakes and light fruitcakes, where it is important to get an even rise, it is best to use self-rising flour because, since the leavening agent has already been added, there is no danger of using too much—which can result in a sunken cake with a poor taste. There are other leavening agents that are used. Some cakes use baking soda with or without cream of tartar (both these compounds are ingredients in baking powder), blended with warm or sour milk. Whisked eggs also act as a leavening agent because the air trapped in the egg ensures that the mixture rises. Generally, no other leavening agent is required.

There is even a special light sponge flour designed especially for beaten sponges. Also, it is possible to buy flours that contain no gluten and, therefore, are suitable for celiacs. Buckwheat, soy, rice and chickpea flours are also available.

Eggs

One of the most versatile ingredients that a cook can use, eggs are particularly important in many baking recipes, from binding doughs to lightening breads and cakes to using as a glaze for breads and rolls. Most eggs sold in the grocery stores are from chickens, and the USDA (United States Department of Agriculture) has established a grading system for them, with higher-quality eggs having yolks that were round and firm and whites that were thick at the time the eggs were laid. AA, A, and B are the grades, with AA being of the best quality, although there is only a slight difference between AA and A. The egg carton should also have a date. To determine if an egg is fresh enough to use, you can put it in a bowl of cold water; if it floats, the egg inside has shrunk and should not be used.

When a recipe states 1 egg, it is generally accepted this refers to a large egg, the size of egg most often used. A large egg weighs 2 ounces, with 1 large egg white equal to 2 tablespoons and 1 large egg yolk equal to 1 tablespoon. Other egg sizes are: jumbo (2½ ounces), extra-large (2¼ ounces), medium (1¾ ounces), and small (1½ ounces). As a guide, if you don't have large eggs and a recipe calls for: 1 large egg, you can use 1 egg of another size; 2 large eggs, substitute 3 small eggs or 2 eggs of another size; 3 large eggs, substitute 2 jumbo eggs, 3 extra-large or medium eggs, or 4 small eggs; 4 large eggs, substitute 3 jumbo eggs, 4 extra-large eggs, or 5 medium or small eggs.

There are many types of eggs sold and it really is a question of personal preference when it comes to which ones are chosen. Whether the shells are brown, white, or even green or blue, all offer the same nutritional benefits. The color of the egg yolk will depend on the diet the hen has been fed on, so wheat-fed hens lay eggs with darker yolks, and feeds of alfalfa, corn, and grass lead to eggs with lighter yolks. It is commonly thought that free-range eggs are from hens that lead a much more natural life and are fed natural foods. This, however, is not always the case—there are no USDA standards—and, in some instances, they may still live in a crowded environment and be fed the same foods as caged hens. Eggs labeled "barn-roaming" are from chickens confined to a barn but that are not caged. Organic eggs are from hens that live in a flock, whose beaks are not clipped, and who are completely free to roam. Obviously, these eggs are much more expensive than the others.

Store eggs in the refrigerator with the round end uppermost (as packaged in the egg cartons). Let them come to room temperature before using. Do remember that you should not give raw or semicooked eggs to babies, toddlers, pregnant women, the elderly, and those with a chronic illness. Consider using pasteurized liquid eggs, found in the refrigerated section in most grocery stores. There are about 4½ eggs in an 8-ounce carton.

When separating eggs (that is, separating the white from the yolk), crack an egg in half lightly and cleanly over a bowl, being careful not to break the yolk and keeping the yolk in the shell. Then tip the yolk backward and forward between the two shell halves, letting as much of the white as possible spill into the bowl. Keep or discard the yolk and/or the white as needed. Make sure that you do not get any yolk in your whites because this will prevent successful whisking of the whites. It takes practice!

Sugar

Sugar not only offers taste to baking but also adds texture and volume to the mixture. Superfine sugar is best for sponge cakes, puddings, and meringues. Its fine granules disperse evenly when creaming or beating. Granulated sugar is used for more general cooking, such as stewing fruit, but can be used as a substitute for superfine sugar. Raw sugar, with its toffee taste and crunchy texture, is good for sticky desserts and cakes, such as oat bars. For rich cakes, such as fruitcake, use brown sugar, which adds a rich, intense molasses flavor.

Confectioners' sugar, also called powdered sugar, is used primarily for frostings and icings and can be used in meringues and in fruit sauces when the sugar needs to dissolve quickly.

You can flavor your own sugar, for example, with vanilla. Place a vanilla bean in a screw-top jar, fill with superfine sugar, screw on the lid, and let stand for 2–3 weeks before using. Top off with more sugar after using it. You can also use thinly pared lemon or orange zest in the same way.

If trying to reduce sugar intake, then use the unrefined varieties, such as unbleached granulated, unbleached superfine, unrefined raw and brown sugar. All of these are a little sweeter than their refined counterparts, so less is required. Alternatively, honey or fructose (fruit sugar) can reduce sugar intake because they have similar calories to sugar, but are twice as sweet. Also, they have a slow release, so their effect lasts longer. Dried fruits can also be included in the diet to top off sugar intake.

Yeast

There is something very comforting about the aroma of freshly baked bread and the taste is far different and superior to commercially made bread. Bread making is regarded by some as being a time-consuming process but, with the advent of fast-acting yeast, this no longer applies. There are three types of yeast available: fresh compressed yeast, granular active dry yeast, and rapid-rise yeast powder, which comes packed in envelopes.

Fresh yeast is rarely sold today as a compressed cake. Commercial baker's yeast is now sold in a liquid form and is not easily available for the general public to buy. If you do manage to find fresh compressed yeast, it should be bought in small quantities (although it freezes well); it has a puttylike color and texture with a slight winelike smell. It should be creamed with a little sugar and some warm liquid before being added to the flour. If you have liquid yeast, just sprinkle on sugar and stir. Dried yeast is much easier to find and use.

Active dry yeast can be stored for up to six months and comes in small hard granules. It should be sprinkled onto lukewarm liquid with a little sugar, then left to stand, normally between 15–20 minutes, until the mixture froths. When replacing fresh yeast with active dry yeast, use 1 tablespoon of active dry yeast for 1 cake fresh compressed yeast.

Rapid-rise yeast (sometimes referred to as "instant," "fast-action," or "easy-blend" yeast) cuts down the time of bread making because it eliminates the need for letting the bread rise twice and can be added straight to the flour without it needing to be activated. When using rapid-rise yeast instead of active-dry yeast, follow recipes that specifically use rapid-rise yeast. When using yeast, the most important thing to remember is that yeast is a living organism and needs food, water, and warmth to work.

Equipment

Nowadays, you can get lost in the cookware sections of some of the larger stores—they really are a cook's paradise with gadgets, cooking tools, and state-of-the-art electronic blenders, mixers, and liquidizers. A few well-picked, high-quality utensils and pieces of equipment will be frequently used and will, therefore, be a much wiser buy than cheaper gadgets.

Cooking equipment not only assists in the kitchen, but can make all the difference between success and failure. Take the humble cake pan: although a very basic piece of cooking equipment, it plays an essential role in baking. Using the incorrect size can mean disaster—a pan that is too large, for example, will spread the mixture too thinly and the result will be a flat, limp-looking cake. On the other hand, cramming the mixture into a pan that is too small will result in the mixture rising up and out of the pan.

Baking Pans & Utensils

To ensure successful baking, it is worth investing in a selection of high-quality pans, which, if looked after properly, should last for many years. Choose heavy-duty metal pans that will not buckle or the new flexible silicone pans—these are easy to turn out, most need very little greasing for a perfect

shape, and they also wash and dry easily. Follow the manufacturer's instructions when first using and ensure that the pans are thoroughly washed and dried after use and before putting away.

Perhaps the most useful of pans for baking are layer cake pans, ideal for classics such as a layer sponge cake, Genoese cake, and coffee and walnut cake. You will need two pans, normally 7 inches or 8 inches in diameter and about 2–3 inches deep. They are often nonstick.

With deep cake pans, it is personal choice whether you buy round or square pans and they vary in size from 5–14 inches (a general useful size is 8 inches), with a depth of between 5 inches and 6 inches. A deep cake pan, for a special fruitcake or a Madeira cake, is a must.

Loaf pans are used for bread, fruit breads, or quick breads and for terrines, and normally come in two sizes: 8 x 4 x 2 inches and 9 x 5 x 3 inches.

Good baking pans and cookie (or baking) sheets are a must for all cooks. Dishes that are too hot to handle, such as apple pies, should be placed directly onto a cookie sheet. Meringues and cookies are cooked on cookie sheets. The difference between baking *pans* and cookie *sheets* is that the former have raised sides all around, whereas cookie sheets have only one raised side, or none.

Square or oblong shallow baking pans, such as jelly roll pans, are also very useful for making sheet cakes, fudge brownies, oat bars, and shortbread. Then there are muffin pans, which are ideal for making muffins, tartlets, or mince pies; and tart pans. They are available in a variety of sizes.

There are plenty of other pans to choose from, ranging from themed pans, such as Christmas tree shapes, numbers from 1–9, and pans shaped as petals, to tube pans (ring-shaped pans

with a hole in the center) and springform pans, where the clips on the sides are released after cooking, so that the finished cake can be removed easily.

A selection of different-size roasting pans (basically deep baking pans) are also a worthwhile investment because they can double up as a bain-marie, or for cooking larger quantities of cakes, such as gingerbread. A few different pans, pie plates, and dishes are required if baking crisps, soufflés, and pies. Custard cups and small ovenproof dishes can be used for a variety of different recipes, as can small tartlet pans and dariole molds.

Another piece of equipment that is worth having is a wire cooling rack. It is essential when baking to let cookies

and cakes cool (in their pans and/or after being removed from their pans), and a wire rack protects your kitchen surfaces from the heat as well as letting air circulate around the goodies, speeding cooling and preventing the base from becoming soggy.

When purchasing your implements for baking, perhaps the rolling pin is one of the most important. Ideally, it should be long and thin, and heavy enough to roll the pastry out easily but not too heavy that it is uncomfortable to use. Pastry needs to be rolled out on a flat surface and, although a lightly floured flat surface will do, a marble slab will ensure that the pastry is kept cool and that the fats do not melt while being rolled. This helps to keep the pastry light, crisp, and flaky instead of heavy, which happens if the fat melts before being baked.

Other useful basic pastry implements are tools such as a pastry brush (which can be used to wet pastry or brush on a glaze), a pastry wheel for cutting, a strainer to remove impurities, and a sifter to sift air into the flour, encouraging the pastry or mixture to be lighter in texture.

Basic mixing cutlery is also essential, such as a wooden spoon (for mixing and creaming), a spatula (for transferring the mixture from the mixing bowl to the baking pans and spreading the mixture once it is in the pans) and a metal spatula (to ease cakes and breads out of their pans before placing them on the wire racks to cool). Measuring pitchers, measuring spoons, and measuring cups are essential for accurate measuring of both dry and wet ingredients. Three to four different sizes of mixing bowls are also very useful.

Electrical Equipment

Nowadays, help from time-saving gadgets and electrical equipment makes baking far easier and quicker. Equipment can be used for creaming, mixing, beating, whisking, kneading, grating, and chopping. There is a wide choice of machines available, from the most basic to the very sophisticated.

Food Processors

When choosing a machine, first decide what you need your processor to do. If you are a novice to baking, it may be a waste to start with a machine that offers a wide range of implements and functions. This can be a deterrent and can result in not using the machine as much as you should. In general, while styling and product design play a role in the price, the more you pay, the larger the machine will be with a bigger bowl capacity and many more gadgets attached. Nowadays, you can chop, shred, slice, chip, blend, puree, knead, whisk, and cream anything. Just what basic features should you ensure your machine has before buying it?

When buying a food processor, look for measurements on the side of the processor bowl and machines with a removable feed tube, which lets you add food or liquid while the motor is still running. Look for machines that have the facility to increase the capacity of the bowl (ideal when making soup) and have a pulse button for controlled chopping. For many, storage is also an issue, so reversible disks and cord storage, or, on more advanced models, a blade storage compartment or box, can be advantageous.

It is also worth thinking about machines that offer optional extras that can be bought as your cooking requirements change. Mini chopping bowls are available for those wanting to chop small quantities of food. If time is an issue, dishwasher-friendly attachments may be vital. Citrus presses, liquidizers, and beaters may all be useful attachments for the cook.

Blenders

Blenders often come as attachments to food processors and are generally used for liquidizing and pureeing foods. There are two main types of blender.

The first is known as a goblet blender. The blades of this blender are at the bottom of the goblet with measurements up the sides. The second blender is portable. It is handheld and should be placed in a bowl to blend.

Food Mixers

These are ideally suited to mixing cakes and kneading dough, either as a tabletop mixer or a handheld mixer. Both are extremely useful and based on the same principle of mixing or beating in an open bowl to get more air into the mixture and, therefore, produce a lighter texture.

The tabletop mixers are freestanding and are capable of dealing with fairly large quantities of mixture. They are robust machines that cope easily with kneading dough and heavy cake mixing as well as whipping cream, whisking egg whites, or making one-stage cakes. These mixers also offer a wide range of attachments, from liquidizers and juicers, to can openers and grinders.

Handheld mixers are smaller than freestanding mixers and often come with their own bowl and stand from which they can be lifted and used as handheld devices. They have a motorized head with detachable twin beaters. These mixers are particularly versatile because they do not need a specific bowl in which to beat. Any suitable mixing bowl can be used.

Basic Techniques

There is no mystery to successful baking—it really is easy, providing you follow a few simple rules and guidelines. First, read the recipe all the way through before commencing. There is nothing more annoying than getting to the middle of a recipe and discovering that you are minus one or two of the ingredients. Until you are confident, follow a recipe; do not try a shortcut, otherwise you may find that you have left out a vital step that means the recipe won't work. Most of all, have patience. Baking is easy—if you can read, you can bake.

Working with Pastry Dough

Pastry dough needs to be kept as cool as possible throughout. Cool hands help, but are not essential. Use cold or iced water, but not too much because the dough does not need to be wet. Be sure that your fat is not runny or melted, but firm (this is why block fat is the best). Avoid using too much flour when rolling out because this alters the proportions, and also avoid handling the dough too much. Chill dough, wrapped in aluminum foil or a plastic bag, for 30 minutes after making it. Roll in one direction to ensure that the dough does not shrink. Let the pastry rest, preferably in the refrigerator, after rolling. If you follow these guidelines but your pastry is still not as good as you would like it to be, then make in a processor instead.

Lining a Tart Pan

It is important to choose the right pan or dish to bake with. You will often find that a loose-bottom metal tart pan is the best option because it conducts heat more efficiently and evenly than a ceramic dish. It also has the added advantage of a removable bottom, which makes the transfer of the baked flan or tart a much simpler process; it simply lifts out, keeping the pastry intact.

Roll the pastry dough out on a lightly floured surface, ensuring that it is a few inches larger than the tart pan. Wrap the dough around the rolling pin, lift, and place in the pan. Carefully ease the dough into the bottom and sides of the pan, ensuring that there are no gaps or tears in the pastry dough. Let rest for a few minutes, then trim the edge either with a sharp knife or by rolling a rolling pin across the top of the tart pan. Prick the pastry dough with the tines of a fork to prevent it from rising up during baking, and chill before baking.

Baking Blind

The term "baking blind" refers to baking the pastry shell without the filling, resulting in a crisp pastry shell that is either partially or completely cooked, depending on if the filling needs cooking. Pastry shells can be prepared ahead of time because they last for several days stored in an airtight container, or longer if frozen.

To bake blind, line a pan or dish with the prepared pastry dough and let it rest in the refrigerator for 30 minutes. This will help to minimize shrinkage while it is being cooked. Remove from the refrigerator and lightly prick the bottom all over with a fork (do not do this if the filling is runny). Simply line the shell with a large square of wax paper, big enough to cover both the bottom and sides of the pastry shell. Fill with pie weights, dried beans, or uncooked rice. Place on a baking sheet and bake in a preheated oven, generally at 400°F, remembering that ovens can take at least 15 minutes to reach this heat (unless they are convection ovens, see page 13). Cook for 10–12 minutes, then remove from the oven, discarding the paper and beans. Return to the oven and continue to cook for an additional 5–10 minutes, depending on whether or not the filling needs cooking. Normally, unless otherwise stated, individual pastry tartlet shells also benefit from baking blind.

Covering a Pie with a Pastry Lid

To cover a pie, roll out the pastry dough until it is about 2 inches larger than the circumference of the dish. Cut a 1-inch strip from around the outside of the pastry dough and then moisten the edge of the pie dish you are using. Place the strip on the edge of the dish and brush with water or beaten egg. Generously fill the pie dish until the

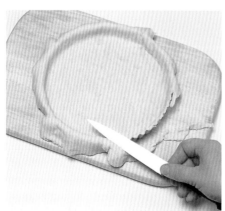

surface is slightly rounded. Using the rolling pin, lift the remaining pastry and cover the pie plate. Press together, then seal. Using a sharp knife, trim off any excess pastry dough from around the edges. Try to avoid brushing the edges of the pastry dough, especially puff pastry, because this prevents the pastry from rising evenly. Before placing in the oven, make a small hole in the center of the pie to let the steam escape.

The edges of the pie can be decorated by pressing the back of a fork around the edge of the pie, or crimp by pinching the edge of the dough, holding the thumb and index finger of one hand against the edge while gently pushing with the index finger of your other hand. Other ways of finishing the pie can be achieved by gently pressing your index finger down onto the rim and, at the same time, tapping a knife horizontally along the edge, giving it a flaky appearance, or by fluting the edges by pressing your thumb down on the edge of the pastry while gently drawing back an all-purpose knife about ½ inch and repeating around the rim. Experiment by putting leaves and berries made out of leftover dough to finish off the pie, then brush the top of the pie with beaten egg.

Greasing and Lining Pans

Most pans will at least need oiling or greasing with butter (butter is better because oil runs off lining paper). If a recipe states that the pan needs lining, do not be tempted to ignore this. Rich fruitcakes and other cakes that take a long time to cook benefit from the pan being lined so that the edges and bottom do not burn or dry out. Wax paper or parchment paper is ideal for this. It is a good idea to use at least a double thickness of the paper, or

preferably 3–4 thicknesses. Sponge cakes and other cakes that are cooked in 30 minutes or less are also better if the bottoms are lined because it is far easier to remove them from the pan.

The best way to line a round or square pan is to draw lightly around the bottom and then cut just inside the markings, making it easy to sit in the pan. Next, lightly grease the paper (with butter) so that it will easily peel away from the cake. If the sides of the pan also need to be lined, then cut a strip of paper long enough to fit the circumference of the pan. This can be measured by wrapping a piece of string around the rim of the pan. Once again, lightly grease the paper, push against the pan, and grease once more because this will hold the paper to the sides of the pan. Steamed puddings usually need only a disk of wax paper at the bottom of the dish so that it will turn out easily.

Hints for Successful Baking

Ensure that the ingredients are accurately measured. A cake that has too much flour or insufficient egg will be dry and crumbly. Be careful when measuring the leavening agent if used, because too much will mean that the cake will rise too quickly and then sink. Insufficient leavening agent means the cake will not rise adequately.

Ensure that the oven is preheated to the correct temperature; it can take 10 minutes to reach up to 375°F, and 15 minutes for above that; however, ovens vary. You may find that an oven thermometer is a good investment. Cakes are best if cooked in the center of the preheated oven. Do try to avoid the temptation of opening the oven door at the beginning of cooking, because a draft of cool air can make the cake sink. Important: If using a convection oven, refer to the manufacturer's instructions, because they normally cook hotter—and faster and more evenly—than conventional ovens and often do not need preheating. As a general rule, set the temperature for a convection oven at

25°F lower than the temperature given in a recipe for a nonconvection oven.

Check that the cake is thoroughly cooked by removing it from the oven and inserting a clean skewer into the cake for 30 seconds before removing it. If the skewer is completely clean, then the cake is cooked; if there is a little mixture left on the skewer, then return to the oven for a few minutes.

Other problems that you may encounter while making a cake are insufficient creaming of the fat and sugar or a curdled creamed mixture (which will result in a densely textured and often solid cake). Flour that has not been folded in carefully enough or that has not been mixed with enough leavening agent may also result in a somewhat heavy consistency. It is important to try to ensure that the correct size of pan is used, because you may end up either with a flat, hard cake or one that has spilled over the edge of the pan. Another thing to be aware of (especially when cooking with fruit) is that, if the consistency is too soft, the cake will not be able to support the fruit.

Finally, when you take your cake out of the oven, unless the recipe states that it should be left in the pan until cold, let it stand for a few minutes to settle, then loosen the edges and turn out onto a wire rack to cool. Cakes that are left in the pan for too long will develop a damp, soggy base.

When storing, make sure the cake is completely cold before placing it into an airtight plastic container. Generally, cookies and cakes will keep for about 5 days in an airtight container. However, if a cake uses fresh cream, cream cheese frosting, or other fresh ingredients, such as fruit, it will last for only 1–2 days if kept refrigerated (note: do not refrigerate cakes covered with sugarpaste). Cakes with buttercream and similar frostings will keep for 2–3 days in a cool place. Light fruitcakes, such as Almond Fruitcake, will store for about a week, and rich fruitcakes, such as Christmas Cake will keep for up to 3 months if fortified with alcohol and wrapped tightly in aluminum foil.

Culinary Terms Explained

At a glance, here are some of the key terms you will come across when baking. Some we may have discussed already, some may be new to you.

Parchment paper Sometimes called "silicone-coated paper," "nonstick baking paper," or "baking parchment." Used for wrapping food to be cooked (en papillote) and for lining cake pans to prevent sticking. Because it is sold as "nonstick," this, in theory, avoids the need to grease or oil the paper.

Wax paper Paper that tends to be relatively nonstick and which is used to line pans for cakes and puddings, but it is advisable to lightly grease this paper to prevent sticking. It is ideal for wrapping food, such as packed lunches or fatty foods. Today, wax paper and parchment paper are often able to be used in the same way—check the packaging.

En papillote A French term used to describe food that is baked, but is wrapped in parchment paper before cooking. This works well with fish because the aroma from the different herbs or spices and the fish are contained during cooking and not released until the paper bundle is opened.

Rice paper This edible paper is made from the pith of a Chinese tree and can be used as a base on which to bake delicate or sticky cakes and cookies, such as almond macaroons.

Baking blind The method often used for cooking the pastry shell of flans and tarts before the filling is added. After lining the pan with the uncooked pastry, it is then covered with a sheet of wax paper or parchment paper and weighed down with pie weights, dried beans, or uncooked rice, and is baked in the oven as directed in the recipe.

Baking powder A leavening agent that works by producing carbon dioxide as a consequence of a reaction caused by the acid and alkali ingredients, which expand during the baking process and make the breads and cakes rise.

Baking soda This alkali powder acts as a leavening agent in baking when combined with an acid or acid liquid (cream of tartar, lemon juice, yogurt, buttermilk, cocoa, or vinegar, for example).

Cream of tartar An acid leavening agent (potassium hydrogen tartrate) often present in self-rising flour and baking powder. Activates the alkali component of baking powder.

Fermenting A term used during bread-, beer-, or winemaking to note the chemical change brought about through the use of a fermenting or leavening agent, such as yeast.

Unleavened Often refers to bread that does not use a leavening agent and is, therefore, flat, such as naan.

Cornstarch Used to thicken consistency and can also be used in making meringue to prevent the meringue from becoming hard and brittle and to enhance its chewiness.

Curdling When the milk separates from a sauce through acidity or

excessive heat. This can also happen to creamed cake mixtures that have separated due to the eggs being too cold or added too quickly.

Sifting The shaking of dry ingredients (primarily flour) through a metal or nylon strainer to remove lumps and impurities, and to add air.

Binding Adding liquid or egg to bring a dry mixture together. Normally, this entails using a fork, spoon, or your fingertips.

Blending When two or more ingredients are thoroughly mixed together.

Creaming The method in which fat and sugar are beaten together until lighter in color and fluffy. By creaming the fat in cake mixtures, air is incorporated into the fairly high fat content. It, thus, lightens the texture of cakes and puddings.

Folding A method of combining creamed fat and sugar with flour in cake and pudding mixes, usually by carefully mixing with a large metal spoon, either by cutting and folding, or by doing a figure-eight in order to maintain a light texture.

Rubbing in The method of combining fat with flour by rubbing them together using your hands. For crumble toppings, flaky pastry dough, cookies, and biscuits.

Beating The method by which air is introduced into a mixture using a fork, wooden spoon, or electric mixer. Beating is also used as a method to soften ingredients.

Whipping/whisking The term given to incorporating air rapidly into a mixture (either through using a manual whisk or an electric mixer).

Dropping consistency The consistency to which a cake or pudding mixture reaches before being cooked. It tends to be fairly soft (but not runny) and should drop off a spoon in around 5 seconds when tapped lightly on the side of a bowl.

Grinding Reducing hard ingredients, such as nuts, to crumbs, normally by the use of a grinder or a mortar and pestle.

Blender An electric machine with rotating blades used mainly with soft and wet ingredients to purée and liquidize, although it can grind dry ingredients, such as nuts and breadcrumbs.

Knead The process of stretching, pummeling, and working dough in order to strengthen the gluten in the flour and make the dough more elastic, thus producing a good rise. Also applies to making pastry; the dough is kneaded on a lightly floured surface to create a smooth and elastic pastry, making it easier to roll and ensuring an even texture after baking. In both cases, the outside of the dough is drawn into the center.

Rising The term used in making bread when letting the bread rest to rise a second time after it has been kneaded once and then shaped before it is baked.

Punched down The term used for a second kneading after the dough has risen. This is done to ensure an even texture and to disperse any large pockets of air.

Crumb The internal texture of a cake or bread as defined by the air pockets.

En croute Used to describe food which is covered with raw pastry and then baked.

Vol-au-vent Translated, it means "to fly or float on the wind." This small and usually round or oval puff pastry shell is first baked and then filled with a savory meat, seafood, or vegetable filling in a sauce.

Choux A type of pastry, whose uncooked dough is somewhat like a glossy batter, which is piped into small balls onto a baking sheet and baked until light and airy. They can then be filled with cream or savory fillings.

Phyllo A type of pastry that is wafer thin. Three to four sheets are usually used at a time, buttered, then layered.

Puff pastry Probably the richest of pastries, because it is enriched with a high proportion of butter, which makes a pastry with light flaky layers. When making from the beginning, it requires the lightest of handling.

Brioche A sweet, spongy traditional bread eaten in France for breakfast, often served warm. Brioche is enriched with eggs and butter and has a rich but soft texture, made from a very light yeast dough, and is baked in the shape of a small cottage loaf. A delicious substitute for bread in bread and butter pudding.

Caramel Obtained by heating sugar on a very low heat until it turns liquid and deep brown in color. This is used in dishes such as crème caramel, which is, in turn, baked in a *bain-marie*.

Bain-marie A French term meaning "water bath." A shallow pan, often a roasting pan, is filled halfway with water; smaller dishes of food are then placed in it, so that they can be cooked at lower temperatures without overheating. This method is often used to cook custards and other egg dishes or to keep some dishes warm.

Custard cup Or ramekin, an ovenproof ceramic dish that provides an individual serving.

Cocotte Another name for a custard cup (a small, ovenproof ceramic dish used for individual portions).

Dariole A small, narrow mold with sloping sides used for making Madeleines. Darioles can also be used for individual steamed or baked puddings and gelatins.

Dusting To sprinkle lightly, often with flour, sugar, or cocoa.

Dredging The sprinkling of food with a coating (generally of flour or sugar). A board may be dredged with flour before the pastry is rolled out, and cakes and cookies can be dredged with sugar or cocoa after baking.

Glacé A French term meaning "glossy" or "iced". Using a glacé, or glaze, is a quick way to decorate cakes and cookies with icing. It is made with confectioners' sugar and water.

Piping A way in which cakes and desserts are decorated, or the method by which choux pastry is placed onto a baking sheet. This is achieved by putting cream, frosting, or another mixture in a nylon bag (with a tip attached), or in an improvised pastry bag made from a cone of wax paper, and then slowly forcing through the tip and piping it onto the cake or baking sheet.

Zest This can refer to the outer, colored part of an orange, lemon, or lime peel, or the very thin, long pieces of that peel (rind). The zest contains the fruit oil, which is responsible for the citrus flavor. Normally, a zester is used to create the strips, because it removes the zest without any of the bitter white pith. Zest can also be grated on a grater into very small pieces, but be careful to remove only the very outer layer.

Everyday Cakes

The following section enables you to prepare a range of popular cakes by simply following the step-by-step instructions and clear picture guides. From the classic Baked Lemon & Golden Raisin Cheesecake to the refreshingly contemporary Cappuccino Cakes, there are recipes to tempt every taste.

Apple & Cinnamon Crumb Cake

INGREDIENTS

Cuts into 8 slices

For the topping:

³/₄ lb. apples, peeled

1 tbsp. lemon juice

1 cup self-rising flour

1 tsp. ground cinnamon

6 tbsp. butter or margarine

6 tbsp. brown sugar

1 tbsp. milk

For the base:

¹/₂ cup (1 stick) butter or margarine

4 tbsp. superfine sugar

2 large eggs

1 cup plus 3 tbsp. self-rising flour

cream or freshly made custard sauce,
    to serve

1. Preheat the oven to 350°F. Lightly grease and line the base of an 8-inch round cake pan with wax paper or parchment paper.

2. Finely chop the apples and mix with the lemon juice. Set aside while making the cake.

3. For the crumble topping, sift the flour and cinnamon together into a large bowl.

4. Rub the butter or margarine into the flour and cinnamon until the mixture resembles coarse bread crumbs.

5. Stir the brown sugar into the bread crumbs and set aside.

6. For the base, cream the butter or margarine and sugar together until light and fluffy. Gradually beat the eggs into the sugar-and-butter mixture a little at a time until all the egg has been added.

7. Sift the flour, and gently fold in with a metal spoon or rubber spatula.

8. Spoon into the base of the prepared cake pan. Arrange the apple pieces on top, then lightly stir the milk into the crumble mixture.

9. Sprinkle the crumble over the apples, and bake in the preheated oven for 1¹/₂ hours. Serve cold with cream or custard sauce.

TASTY TIP

For a crunchier-textured topping, stir in ¹/₂ cup of chopped mixed nuts and seeds to the crumble mixture in step 5.

2

6

9

Chocolate & Coconut Cake

INGREDIENTS

Cuts into 8 slices

4 oz. semisweet dark chocolate,
  roughly chopped
³/₄ cup (1¹/₂ sticks) butter or
  margarine
²/₄ superfine sugar
3 large eggs, beaten
1¹/₂ cups self-rising flour
1 tbsp. cocoa
³/₄ cup unsweetened shredded
  dry coconut

For the frosting:

¹/₂ cup (1 stick) butter or margarine
2 tbsp. creamed coconut
2 cups confectioners' sugar
¹/₃ cup lightly toasted unsweetened
  shredded dry coconut

TASTY TIP

Why not experiment with the chocolate in this recipe? For a different taste, try using orange-flavored dark chocolate or add 1–2 tablespoons of rum when melting the chocolate.

1 Preheat the oven to 350°F. Melt the chocolate in a small bowl placed over a saucepan of gently simmering water, making sure that the base of the bowl does not touch the water. When the chocolate has melted, stir until smooth and let cool.

2 Lightly grease and line the bases of two 7-inch round cake pans with parchment paper. In a large bowl, beat the butter or margarine and sugar together with a wooden spoon until light and creamy. Beat in the eggs a little at a time, then stir in the melted chocolate.

3 Sift the flour and cocoa together and gently fold into the chocolate mixture with a metal spoon or rubber spatula. Add the shredded coconut and mix lightly. Divide between the two prepared pans and smooth the tops.

4 Bake in the preheated oven for 25–30 minutes or until a skewer comes out clean when inserted into the center of the cake. Let cool in the pan for 5 minutes, then turn out, discard the lining paper, and leave on a wire rack until cool.

5 Beat together the butter or margarine and creamed coconut until fluffy. Add the confectioners' sugar and mix well. Spread half of the frosting on one layer and press the cakes together. Spread the remaining frosting over the top, sprinkle with the shredded coconut, and serve.

1

4

5

Victoria Sponge with Mango & Mascarpone

INGREDIENTS

Cuts into 8 slices

¾ cup superfine sugar, plus extra
   for dusting

1½ cups self-rising flour, plus extra
   for dusting

¾ cup (1½ sticks) butter or margarine

3 extra-large eggs

1 tsp. vanilla extract

2 ½ tbsp. confectioners' sugar

9 oz. mascarpone cheese

1 large ripe mango, peeled

TASTY TIP

Mango has been used in this recipe, but mashed strawberries could be used instead. Set aside a few whole strawberries, slice, and use to decorate the cake.

1 Preheat the oven to 375°F. Lightly grease two 7-inch layer-cake pans, and lightly dust with superfine sugar and flour, tapping the pans to remove any excess.

2 In a large bowl, cream the butter or margarine and sugar together with a wooden spoon until light and creamy.

3 In another bowl, mix the eggs and vanilla extract together. Sift the flour several times onto a plate.

4 Beat a little egg into the butter and sugar, then add a little flour and beat well.

5 Continue adding the flour and eggs alternately, beating between each addition until the mixture is well mixed and smooth. Divide the mixture between the 2 prepared cake pans, level the surface, then using the back of a large spoon, make a slight dip in the center of each cake.

6 Bake in the preheated oven for 25–30 minutes until the center of the cake springs back when gently pressed with a clean finger. Turn out onto a wire rack and leave the cakes until cool.

7 Beat the confectioners' sugar and mascarpone cheese together, then chop the mango into small cubes.

8 Use half the mascarpone and mango to sandwich the cakes together. Spread the rest of the mascarpone on top, decorate with the remaining mango, and serve. Otherwise, lightly cover and store in the refrigerator. Use within 3–4 days.

1

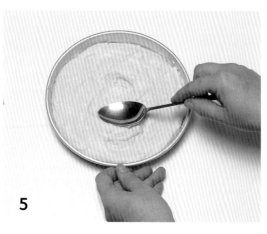

5

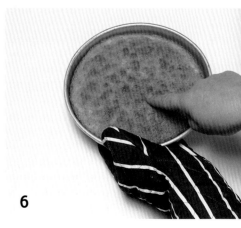

6

Almond Cake

INGREDIENTS

Cuts into 8 slices

1 cup (2 sticks) butter or margarine

1 cup superfine sugar

3 extra-large eggs

1 tsp. vanilla extract

1 tsp. almond extract

1 cup self-rising flour

1½ cups ground almonds

⅓ cup blanched whole almonds

1 square semisweet chocolate

TASTY TIP

Baking with ground almonds helps to keep the cake moist as well as adding a slight nutty flavor to the cake. Add 1–2 tablespoons of orange juice with the zest of an orange in step 4 if a fragrant citrus flavor is desired, but omit the vanilla extract.

1   Preheat the oven to 300°F. Lightly grease and line the base of an 8-inch round cake pan with wax paper or parchment paper.

2   Cream together the butter or margarine and sugar with a wooden spoon until light and fluffy.

3   Beat the eggs and extracts together in a small bowl. Gradually add to the sugar and butter mixture, and mix well between each addition.

4   Sift the flour, and mix with the ground almonds. Beat into the egg mixture until mixed well and smooth. Pour into the prepared cake pan. Roughly chop the whole almonds, and sprinkle over cake before baking.

5   Bake in the preheated oven for 45 minutes or until golden and risen, and a skewer inserted into the center of the cake comes out clean.

6   Remove from the pan and let cool on a wire rack. Melt the chocolate in a small bowl placed over a saucepan of gently simmering water, stirring until smooth and free of lumps.

7   Drizzle the melted chocolate over the cooled cake, and serve once the chocolate has set.

2

5

8

Lemon Drizzle Cake

INGREDIENTS

Cuts into 16 squares

½ cup (1 stick) butter or margarine
¾ cup superfine sugar
2 extra-large eggs
1½ cups self-rising flour
2 lemons, preferably unwaxed
4 tbsp. granulated sugar

FOOD FACT

This classic cake is a favorite in many kitchens. The buttery sponge cake is perfectly complemented by the lemon syrup, which soaks into the cake, giving it a gooeyness that is even better the next day!

1 Preheat the oven to 350°F. Lightly grease and line the base of a 7-inch square cake pan with nonstick parchment paper.

2 In a large bowl, cream the butter or margarine and superfine sugar together until soft and fluffy.

3 Beat the eggs, then gradually add a little of the egg to the creamed mixture, adding 1 tablespoon of flour after each addition.

4 Finely grate the zest from one of the lemons, and stir into the creamed mixture, beating well until smooth. Squeeze the juice from the lemon, strain, then stir into the mixture.

5 Spoon into the prepared pan, level the surface, and bake in the preheated oven for 25–30 minutes. Using a zester, remove the strips of zest from the remaining lemon, mix with 2 tablespoons of the granulated sugar, and set aside.

6 Squeeze the juice into a small saucepan. Add the rest of the granulated sugar to the lemon juice in the saucepan and heat gently, stirring occasionally.

7 When sugar has dissolved, simmer gently for 3–4 minutes until syrupy.

8 With a toothpick or fine skewer, prick the cake all over.

9 Sprinkle the lemon zest and sugar over the top of the cake, drizzle over the syrup, and allow it cool in the pan. Cut the cake into squares and serve.

3

5

9

Jelly Roll

INGREDIENTS

Cuts into 8 slices

$^3/_4$ cup self-rising flour

3 extra-large eggs

1 tsp. vanilla extract

7 tbsp. superfine sugar

$^1/_4$ cup toasted and finely
  chopped hazelnuts

3 tbsp. apricot preserves

$1^1/_4$ cups lightly whipped heavy cream

TASTY TIP

Any flavor of preserves can be used in this recipe. While apricot preserves are delicious, raspberry or blackberry preserves also work very well. In place of the cream, why not try butter-cream icing or beaten mascarpone as a filling?

1   Preheat the oven to 425°F. Lightly grease and line the base of a 13-inch jelly-roll pan with a single sheet of nonstick parchment paper.

2   Sift the flour several times, then set aside on top of the oven to warm a little.

3   Place a mixing bowl with the eggs, vanilla extract, and sugar over a saucepan of hot water, making sure that the base of the bowl is not touching the water. With the saucepan off the heat, beat with an electric hand mixer until the egg mixture becomes pale and mousselike, and has increased in volume.

4   Remove the basin from the saucepan and continue to beat for an additional 2–3 minutes. Sift in the flour and very gently fold in using a metal spoon or rubber spatula, taking care not to knock out the air beated in already. Pour into the prepared pan, tilting to make sure that the mixture is evenly distributed.

5   Bake in the preheated oven for 10–12 minutes or until well risen, golden brown, and the top springs back when touched lightly with a clean finger.

6   Sprinkle the toasted, chopped hazelnuts over a large sheet of wax paper. When the cake has cooked, turn out onto the nut-covered paper, and trim its edges. Holding an edge of the paper with the short side of the cake nearest you, roll up the cake.

7   When fully cool, carefully unroll and spread with the apricot preserves, and then the cream. Roll back up and serve. Otherwise, store in the refrigerator and eat within two days.

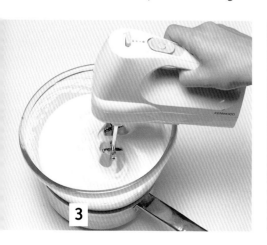

3

6

7

Toffee Apple Cake

INGREDIENTS

Cuts into 8 slices

2 small apples, peeled
4 tbsp. dark brown sugar
$^3/_4$ cup ($1^1/_2$ sticks) butter or margarine
$^3/_4$ cup superfine sugar
3 large eggs
$1^1/_2$ cups self-rising flour
$^2/_3$ cup heavy cream
2 tbsp. confectioners' sugar
$^1/_2$ tsp. vanilla extract
$^1/_2$ tsp. ground cinnamon

1. Preheat the oven to 180°F. Lightly grease and line the bases of two 8-inch layer-cake pans with nonstick parchment paper.

2. Thinly slice the apples and toss in the brown sugar until well coated. Arrange them over the base of the prepared pans, and set aside.

3. Cream together the butter or margarine and superfine sugar until light and fluffy.

4. Beat the eggs together in a small bowl, and gradually beat them into the creamed mixture, beating well between each addition.

5. Sift the flour into the mixture and, using a metal spoon or rubber spatula, fold in.

6. Divide the mixture between the two cake pans and level the surface.

7. Bake in the preheated oven for 25–30 minutes until golden and well risen. Leave in the pans to cool.

8. Lightly whip the cream with 1 tablespoon of the confectioners' sugar and the vanilla extract.

9. Sandwich the cakes together with the cream. Mix the rest of the sugar and ground cinnamon together, sprinkle over the top of the cake, and serve.

TASTY TIP

The dark brown sugar used in this recipe could be replaced with a golden brown sugar to give a deliciously rich toffee flavor to the apples. When baked, the sugar melts into a caramel consistency.

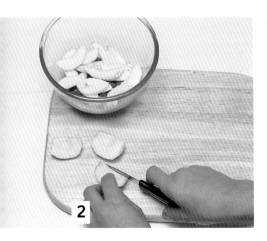

2

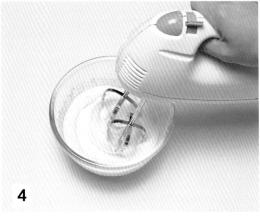

4

9

Cappuccino Cakes

INGREDIENTS

Makes 6

½ cup (1 stick) butter or margarine
½ cup superfine sugar
2 large eggs
1 tbsp. strong black coffee
1½ cups self-rising flour
½ lb. mascarpone cheese
1 tbsp. confectioners' sugar, sifted
1 tsp. vanilla extract
sifted cocoa, to dust

TASTY TIP

The combination of coffee with the vanilla-flavored mascarpone is heavenly! Make sure you use a good-quality coffee in this recipe. Colombian coffee is generally good, and at its best, possesses a smooth, rounded flavor.

1 Preheat the oven to 375°F. Place six large paper baking cups in a muffin pan, or place them on a cookie sheet.

2 Cream the butter or margarine and sugar together until light and fluffy. Break the eggs into a small bowl, and beat lightly with a fork.

3 Using a wooden spoon, beat the eggs into the butter and sugar mixture, a little at a time, until they are all incorporated.

4 If the mixture looks curdled, beat in a spoonful of the flour to return the mixture to a smooth consistency. Finally, beat in the black coffee.

5 Sift the flour into the mixture, then with a metal spoon or rubber spatula, gently fold in the flour.

6 Place spoonfuls of the mixture in the baking cups.

7 Bake in the preheated oven for 20–25 minutes or until risen and springy to the touch. Cool on a wire rack.

8 In a small bowl, beat together the mascarpone cheese, confectioners' sugar, and vanilla extract.

9 When the cakes are cool, spoon the vanilla mascarpone on top. Dust with cocoa and serve. Eat within 24 hours and store in the refrigerator.

4

6

9

Fruitcake

INGREDIENTS

Cuts into 10 slices

1 cup (2 sticks) butter or margarine

scant 1 cup brown sugar

finely grated zest of 1 orange

1 tbsp. molasses

3 extra-large eggs, beaten

2 ½ cups all-purpose flour

¼ tsp. ground cinnamon

½ tsp. pumpkin pie spice

pinch of freshly grated nutmeg

¼ tsp. baking soda

½ cup mixed candied peel

¼ cup candied cherries

⅔ cup raisins

⅔ cup golden raisins

⅔ cup chopped dried apricots

TASTY TIP

For a fruitcake with a kick, remove the cake from the oven when cooked and leave to cool. When the cake has cooled, turn out and make holes in the bottom of the cake with a skewer. Dribble over 4–5 tablespoons of your favorite alcohol such as whisky, brandy, or Drambuie.

1. Preheat the oven to 300°F. Lightly grease and line a 9-inch round cake pan with a double thickness of wax paper.

2. In a large bowl, cream together the butter or margarine, sugar, and orange zest until light and fluffy, then beat in the molasses.

3. Beat in the eggs, a little at a time, beating well between each addition.

4. Set aside 1 tablespoon of the flour. Sift the remaining flour, the spices, and baking soda into the mixture.

5. Mix all the fruits and the remaining flour together, then stir into the cake mixture.

6. Turn into the prepared pan and smooth the top, making a small hollow in the center of the cake mixture.

7. Bake in the preheated oven for 1 hour, then reduce the heat to 275°F.

8. Bake for an additional 1½ hours or until cooked and a skewer inserted into the center comes out clean. Let cool in the pan, then turn the cake out, and serve. Otherwise, when cool, store in an airtight container.

2

5

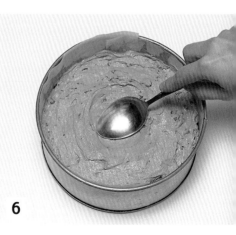

6

Banana Cake

INGREDIENTS

Cuts into 8 slices

3 medium-sized, ripe bananas

1 tsp. lemon juice

$^2/_3$ cup brown sugar

6 tbsp. butter or margarine

2$^1/_4$ cups self-rising flour

1 tsp. ground cinnamon

3 large eggs

$^1/_2$ cup chopped walnuts

1 tsp. each ground cinnamon and
   superfine sugar, to decorate

heavy cream, to serve

HELPFUL HINT

The riper the bananas used in this recipe, the better. This cake tastes really delicious the day after it has been made—the sponge cake solidifies slightly, yet does not lose any moisture. Eat within 3–4 days.

1   Preheat the oven to 375°F. Lightly grease and line the base of a 7-inch round cake pan with wax paper or parchment paper.

2   Mash two of the bananas in a small bowl, sprinkle with the lemon juice and a heaping tablespoon of the sugar. Mix together lightly, and set aside.

3   Gently heat the remaining sugar and butter or margarine in a small saucepan until the butter has just melted.

4   Pour into a small bowl, then allow to cool slightly. Sift the flour and cinnamon into a large bowl and make a well in the center.

5   Beat the eggs into the cooled sugar mixture, pour into the well of flour, and mix thoroughly.

6   Gently stir in the mashed banana mixture. Pour half of the mixture into the prepared pan. Thinly slice the remaining banana, and arrange over the cake mixture.

7   Sprinkle over the chopped walnuts, then cover with the remaining cake mixture.

8   Bake in the preheated oven for 50–55 minutes or until well risen and golden brown. Allow to cool in the pan, turn out, and sprinkle with the cinnamon and superfine sugar. Serve hot or cold with a pitcher of heavy cream for pouring.

2

5

7

Coffee & Pecan Cake

INGREDIENTS

Cuts into 8 slices

1¹/₃ cups self-rising flour
¹/₂ cup (1 stick) butter or margarine
³/₄ cup brown sugar
1 tbsp. instant coffee
2 extra-large eggs
¹/₂ cup roughly chopped pecans

For the frosting:

1 tsp. instant coffee
1 tsp. unsweetened cocoa
6 tbsp. softened unsalted butter
1¹/₂ cups confectioners' sugar, sifted
whole pecans, to decorate

HELPFUL HINT

To enjoy this cake whenever you want, bake in bulk. Follow the recipe to step 5, then when cakes have cooled, wrap in plastic wrap or foil, and freeze. When desired, remove from freezer, loosen wrappings, and allow to defrost slowly at room temperature. Serve with or without frosting.

1 Preheat the oven to 375°F. Lightly grease and line the bases of two 7-inch layer-cake pans with wax paper or parchment paper. Sift the flour and set aside.

2 Beat the butter or margarine and sugar together until light and creamy. Dissolve the coffee in 2 tablespoons of hot water and allow to cool.

3 Lightly mix the eggs with the coffee liquid. Gradually beat into the creamed butter and sugar, adding a little of the sifted flour with each addition.

4 Fold in the pecans, then divide the mixture between the prepared pans, and bake in the preheated oven for 20–25 minutes or until well risen and firm to the touch.

5 Leave in the pans for 5 minutes before turning out and cooling on a wire rack.

6 To make the frosting, blend the coffee and cocoa with enough boiling water to make a stiff paste. Beat into the butter and confectioners' sugar.

7 Sandwich the two cakes together using half of the frosting. Spread the remaining frosting over the top of the cake and decorate with the whole pecans to serve. Store in an airtight container.

3

4

6

Carrot Cake

INGREDIENTS

Cuts into 8 slices

1³/₄ cups all-purpose flour

¹/₂ tsp. ground cinnamon

¹/₂ tsp. freshly grated nutmeg

1 tsp. baking powder

1 tsp. baking soda

²/₃ cup brown sugar

1 scant cup vegetable oil

3 large eggs

¹/₂ lb. peeled and roughly grated
    carrots

¹/₂ cup chopped walnuts

For the frosting:

³/₄ cup cream cheese

finely grated zest of 1 orange

1 tbsp. orange juice

1 tsp. vanilla extract

1 cup confectioners' sugar

TASTY TIP

For a fruitier cake, add 1 grated apple and ¹/₃ cup of golden raisins in step 5. To plump up the raisins, soak for an hour or overnight in a cup of cold tea.

1. Preheat the oven to 300°F. Lightly grease and line the base of a 6-inch square cake pan with wax parchment paper.

2. Sift the flour, spices, baking powder, and baking soda together into a large bowl.

3. Stir in the brown sugar and mix together.

4. Lightly beat the oil and eggs together, then gradually stir into the flour and sugar mixture. Stir well.

5. Add the carrots and walnuts. Mix thoroughly, then pour into the prepared cake pan. Bake in the preheated oven for 1¹/₂ hours or until light and springy to the touch and a skewer inserted into the center of the cake comes out clean.

6. Remove from the oven and allow to cool for 5 minutes before turning out onto a wire rack. Set aside until cool.

7. To make the frosting, beat together the cream cheese, orange zest, orange juice, and vanilla extract. Sift the confectioners' sugar and stir into the cream cheese mixture.

8. When cool, discard the lining paper, spread the cream cheese frosting over the top, and serve cut into squares.

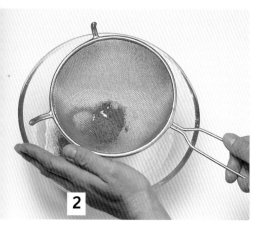
2

5

7

Whisked Sponge Cake

INGREDIENTS

Cuts into 6 slices

1 cup all-purpose flour, plus 1 tsp.

³/₄ cup superfine sugar,
  plus 1 tsp.

3 large eggs

1 tsp. vanilla extract

4 tbsp. raspberry jelly

¹/₂ cup fresh raspberries, crushed

confectioners' sugar, to dust

TASTY TIP

For a creamier, low-fat filling, mix the crushed berries with 4 tablespoons each of low-fat, plain yogurt and low-fat crème fraîche or sour cream.

1   Preheat the oven to 400°F. Mix 1 teaspoon of the flour and 1 teaspoon of the sugar together. Lightly grease two 7-inch layer-cake pans and dust lightly with the sugar and flour mixture.

2   Place the eggs in a large heatproof bowl. Add the sugar, then place over a saucepan of gently simmering water, making sure that the base of the bowl does not touch the hot water. Use an electric mixer to beat the sugar and eggs until they become light and fluffy. (The whisks should leave a trail in the mixture when lifted out.)

3   Remove the bowl from the saucepan of water, add the vanilla extract, and continue beating for 2–3 minutes. Sift the flour gently into the egg mixture and, using a metal spoon or rubber spatula, carefully fold in, taking care not to overmix and remove all the air that has been beaten in.

4   Divide the mixture between the two prepared cake pans. Tap lightly on the work surface to remove any air bubbles. Bake in the preheated oven for 20–25 minutes or until golden. Test that the cake is ready by gently pressing the center with a clean finger—it should spring back.

5   Let cool for 5 minutes, then turn out onto a wire rack. Blend the jelly and the crushed raspberries together. When the cakes are cold, spread over the jelly mixture and sandwich together. Dust the top with confectioners' sugar, and serve.

1

2

5

Marble Cake

INGREDIENTS

Cuts into 8 slices

1 cup (2 sticks) butter or margarine

1 cup superfine sugar

4 large eggs

2 cups self-rising flour, sifted

finely grated zest and juice of
  1 orange

3 tbsp. cocoa, sifted

For the topping:

zest and juice of 1 orange

1 tbsp. granulated sugar

HELPFUL HINT

This cake has a wonderful combination of rich chocolate and orangey sponge. It is important not to swirl too much in step 2, since the desired effect is to have a multicolored cake.

1 Preheat the oven to 375°F. Lightly grease and line the base of an 8-inch round cake pan with wax paper or parchment paper.

2 In a large bowl, cream the butter or margarine and sugar together until light and fluffy.

3 Beat the eggs together. Beat into the creamed mixture, a little at a time, beating well between each addition. When all the egg has been added, fold in the flour with a metal spoon or rubber spatula.

4 Divide the mixture equally between two bowls. Beat the grated orange zest into one of the bowls with a little of the orange juice. Mix the cocoa with the remaining orange juice until smooth, then add to the other bowl and beat well.

5 Spoon the mixture into the prepared pan, in alternate spoonfuls. When all the cake mixture is in the pan, take a skewer and swirl in the two mixtures.

6 Tap the base of the pan on the work surface to level the mixture. Bake in the preheated oven for 50 minutes or until cooked and a skewer inserted into the center of the cake comes out clean.

7 Remove from the oven and leave in the pan for a few minutes before cooling on a wire rack. Discard the lining paper. For the topping, place the orange zest and juice with the granulated sugar in a small saucepan, and heat gently until the sugar has dissolved.

8 Bring to a boil and simmer gently for 3–4 minutes until the juice is syrupy. Pour over the cooled cake, and serve when cool. Otherwise, store the marble cake in an airtight container.

4

5

8

Rich Chocolate Cupcakes

INGREDIENTS

Makes 12

1½ cups self-rising flour
¼ cup unsweetened cocoa
¾ cup golden brown sugar
6 tbsp. melted butter
2 lightly beaten large eggs
1 tsp. vanilla extract
2 tbsp. drained and chopped
   maraschino cherries

For the chocolate frosting:

2 oz. bittersweet dark chocolate
2 tbsp. unsalted butter
¼ cup confectioners' sugar, sifted

For the cherry icing:

1 cup confectioners' sugar
2 tsp. melted unsalted butter
1 tsp. syrup from the
   maraschino cherries
3 maraschino cherries, halved,
   to decorate

1 Preheat the oven to 350°F. Line a 12-cup muffin pan with baking cups. Sift the flour and unsweetened cocoa into a bowl. Stir in the sugar, then add the melted butter, eggs, and vanilla extract. Beat together with a wooden spoon for 3 minutes or until well blended.

2 Divide half the batter among six of the paper cups. Dry the cherries thoroughly on absorbent paper towels, then fold into the remaining mixture and spoon into the rest of the paper cases.

3 Bake on the shelf above the center of the preheated oven for 20 minutes or until a toothpick inserted into the center of a cake comes out clean. Transfer to a wire rack until cool.

4 For the chocolate frosting, melt the chocolate and butter in a heatproof bowl set over a saucepan of hot water. Remove from the heat and let cool for 3 minutes, stirring occasionally. Stir in the confectioners' sugar. Spoon the mixture over the six chocolate cakes and allow to set.

5 For the cherry icing, sift the confectioners' sugar into a bowl and stir in 1 tablespoon of boiling water, the butter, and cherry syrup. Spoon the frosting over the remaining six cakes, decorate each with a halved cherry, and allow to set.

1

3

4

All-in-One Chocolate Fudge Cakes

INGREDIENTS

Cuts into 15 squares

$3/4$ cup firmly packed dark
   brown sugar

$3/4$ cup ($1^1/2$ sticks) butter, softened

$1^1/4$ cups self-rising flour

$1/4$ cup unsweetened cocoa

$1/2$ tsp. baking powder

pinch of salt

3 large eggs, lightly beaten

1 tbsp. corn syrup

For the fudge topping:

$3/4$ cup granulated sugar

$2/3$ cup evaporated milk

6 oz. semisweet dark chocolate,
   coarsely chopped

3 tbsp. unsalted butter, softened

1 cup finely chopped fudge candies

1 Preheat the oven to 350°F. Grease and line a 7 x 11 inch cake pan with nonstick parchment paper.

2 Place the brown sugar and butter in a large bowl, and sift in the flour, unsweetened cocoa, baking powder, and salt. Add the eggs and corn syrup, then beat with an electric whisk for 2 minutes, then add 2 tablespoons of warm water and beat for an additional minute.

3 Turn the batter into the prepared pan and level the top with the back of a spoon. Bake on the center shelf of the preheated oven for 30 minutes or until firm to the touch. Turn the cake out onto a wire rack to cool.

4 To make the topping, gently heat the sugar and evaporated milk in a saucepan, stirring frequently until the sugar has dissolved. Bring the mixture to a boil and simmer for 6 minutes, without stirring.

5 Remove the mixture from the heat. Add the chocolate and butter, and stir until melted and blended. Pour into a bowl and chill in the refrigerator for 1–2 hours or until thickened. Spread the topping over the cake, then sprinkle with the chopped fudge. Cut the cake into 15 squares before serving.

TASTY TIP

Use a mixture of fudge candies for the topping on this cake, including chocolate, vanilla, and caramel flavors.

2

3

5

Orange Chocolate Cheesecake

INGREDIENTS

Cuts into 8 slices

8 graham crackers
4 tbsp. butter
4 cups mixed fruits, such as
  blueberries and raspberries
1 tbsp. confectioners' sugar, sifted
few sprigs of fresh mint, to decorate

For the filling:

2 cups cream cheese
1 tbsp. gelatin
12 oz. orange chocolate, broken
  into segments
2 cups heavy cream

1 Lightly grease and line an 8-inch round springform cake pan with nonstick parchment paper. Place the graham crackers in a plastic container, and crush using a rolling pin. Alternatively, use a food processor. Melt the butter in a medium-sized heavy saucepan, add the crumbs, and mix well. Press the crumb mixture into the bottom of the lined pan, then chill in the refrigerator for 20 minutes.

2 For the filling, allow the cream cheese to come to room temperature. Place the cream cheese in a bowl and beat until smooth, then set aside.

3 Pour 4 tablespoons of water into a small bowl and sprinkle over the gelatin. Allow to stand for 5 minutes until spongy. Place the bowl over a saucepan of simmering water and allow to dissolve, stirring occasionally. Let cool slightly.

4 Melt the orange chocolate in a heatproof bowl set over a saucepan of simmering water, then let cool slightly.

5 Whip the cream until soft peaks form. Beat the gelatin and chocolate into cream cheese. Fold in the cream. Spoon into the pan and level the surface. Chill in the refrigerator for 4 hours until set.

6 Remove the cheesecake from the pan and place on a serving plate. Top with the mixed fruits, dust with sifted confectioners' sugar, and decorate with sprigs of mint.

HELPFUL HINT

Always add gelatin to the mixture you are working with and beat well to evenly distribute it. Never add the mixture to the gelatin or it will tend to set in a lump.

1

5

6

Baked Lemon & Golden Raisin Cheesecake

INGREDIENTS

Cuts into 10 slices

1¼ cups superfine sugar
4 tbsp. butter
½ cup self-rising flour
½ tsp. baking powder
5 extra-large eggs
2 cups cream cheese
4 tbsp. all-purpose flour
grated zest of 1 lemon
3 tbsp. fresh lemon juice
½ cup crème fraîche
½ cup golden raisins

To decorate:

1 tbsp. confectioners' sugar
fresh blueberries
mint leaves

TASTY TIP

Vary the flavor by adding a little freshly grated nutmeg and ½ teaspoon of ground cinnamon to the base in step 2. Add a little of both spices to the confectioners' sugar before sprinkling.

1　Preheat the oven to 325°F. Grease an 8-inch springform cake pan with nonstick parchment paper.

2　Beat 4 tablespoons of the sugar and the butter together until light and creamy, then stir in the self-rising flour, baking powder, and 1 egg.

3　Mix lightly together until well blended. Spoon into the prepared pan and spread the mixture over the base. Separate the four remaining eggs and set aside.

4　Blend the cheese in a food processor until soft. Gradually add the eggs yolks and sugar, and blend until smooth. Turn into a bowl and stir in the rest of the flour, lemon zest, and juice.

5　Mix lightly before adding the crème fraîche and golden raisins, stirring well.

6　Beat the egg whites until stiff, fold into the cheese mixture, and pour into the pan. Tap lightly on the surface to remove any air bubbles. Bake in the preheated oven for about 1 hour or until golden and firm.

7　Cover lightly if browning too much. Turn the oven off and leave in the oven to cool for 2–3 hours.

8　Remove the cheesecake from the oven and, when completely cold, remove from the pan. Sprinkle with the confectioners' sugar, decorate with the blueberries and mint leaves, and serve.

3

4

5

Cakes for Special Occasions

Whether you are planning to amaze your guests or simply wish to indulge yourself, these easy-to-prepare recipes will never fail to impress. This varied selection of delicious cakes ranges from the richly chocolate to the lightly fruity.

Apricot & Almond Layer Cake

INGREDIENTS

Cuts into 8–10 slices

²/₃ cup (1¹/₄ sticks) unsalted
  butter, softened

¹/₂ cup sugar

5 large eggs, separated

5 oz. bittersweet chocolate, melted
  and cooled

1¹/₄ cups self-rising flour, sifted

¹/₂ cup ground almonds

³/₄ cup confectioners' sugar, sifted

³/₄ cup apricot jelly

1 tbsp. amaretto liqueur

For the frosting:

¹/₂ cup (1 stick) unsalted
  butter, melted

4 oz. semisweet dark
  chocolate, melted

1 Preheat the oven to 350°F. Lightly grease and line two 9-inch round cake pans. Cream the butter and sugar together until light and fluffy, then beat in the egg yolks, one at a time, beating well after each addition. Stir in the cooled chocolate with 1 tablespoon of cooled boiled water, then fold in the flour and ground almonds.

2 Beat the egg whites until stiff, then gradually beat in the confectioners' sugar, beating well after each addition. Beat until stiff and glossy, then fold the egg whites into the chocolate mixture in two batches.

3 Divide the batter evenly among the prepared pans and bake in the preheated oven for 30–40 minutes or until firm. Leave for 5 minutes before turning out onto wire racks. Let cool completely.

4 Split the cakes in half. Gently heat the jelly, pass through a strainer, and stir in the amaretto liqueur. Place one cake layer onto a serving plate. Spread with a little of the jelly, then sandwich with the next layer. Repeat with all the layers and use any remaining jelly to brush over the entire cake. Leave until the jelly sets.

5 Meanwhile, to make the frosting, beat the butter and chocolate together until smooth, then cool at room temperature until thick enough to spread. Cover the top and sides of the cake with the chocolate frosting, and let set before slicing and serving.

HELPFUL HINT

Use a very good-quality apricot jelly as it is a major flavor in the finished cake.

1

2

4

Mocha Truffle Cake

INGREDIENTS

Cuts into 8–10 slices

3 large eggs

$^1\!/_2$ cup caster sugar

$^1\!/_3$ cup cornstarch

$^1\!/_3$ cup self-rising flour

2 tbsp. unsweetened cocoa

2 tbsp. milk

2 tbsp. coffee liqueur

$3^1\!/_2$ oz. white chocolate,
   melted and cooled

7 oz. semisweet dark chocolate,
   melted and cooled

2 cups heavy cream

7 oz. milk chocolate

7 tbsp. unsalted butter

1　Preheat the oven to 350°F. Lightly grease and line a deep 9-inch round cake pan. Beat the eggs and sugar in a bowl until thick and creamy.

2　Sift together the cornstarch, self-rising flour, and cocoa, and fold into the egg mixture. Spoon into the prepared pan, and bake in the preheated oven for 30 minutes or until firm. Turn out onto a wire rack and leave until cool. Split the cooled cake horizontally into two layers. Mix together the milk and coffee liqueur, and brush onto the cake layers.

3　Stir the cooled white chocolate into one bowl and the cooled dark chocolate into another one. Whip the cream until soft peaks form, then divide among the two bowls and stir. Place one layer of cake in a 9-inch springform pan. Spread with half the white chocolate cream. Top with the dark chocolate cream, then the remaining white chocolate cream, and finally place the remaining cake layer on top. Chill in the refrigerator for 4 hours or until set.

4　When ready to serve, melt the milk chocolate and butter in a heatproof bowl set over a saucepan of simmering water, and stir until smooth. Remove from the heat and leave until thick enough to spread, then use to cover the top and sides of the cake. Allow to set at room temperature, then chill in the refrigerator. Cut the cake into slices and serve.

HELPFUL HINT

Unless you are going to make a lot of chocolate or coffee desserts, liqueurs are very expensive to buy. Look for generic brands or miniatures.

1

2

3

Chocolate Buttermilk Cake

INGREDIENTS

Cuts into 8–10 slices

³/₄ cup (1¹/₂ sticks) butter

1 tsp. vanilla extract

1¹/₂ cups superfine sugar

4 large eggs, separated

³/₄ cup self-rising flour

¹/₄ cup unsweetened cocoa

¹/₄ cup buttermilk

7 oz. semisweet dark chocolate

7 tbsp. butter

1 cup heavy cream

1 Preheat the oven to 350°F. Lightly grease and line a deep 9-inch round cake pan. Cream together the butter, vanilla extract, and sugar until light and fluffy, then beat in the egg yolks, one at a time.

2 Sift together the flour and cocoa and fold into the egg mixture together with the buttermilk. Beat the egg whites until soft peaks form, and fold carefully into the chocolate mixture in two batches. Spoon the batter into the prepared pan, and bake in the preheated oven for 1 hour or until firm. Cool slightly, then turn out onto a wire rack and leave until completely cooled.

3 Place the chocolate and butter together in a heatproof bowl set over a saucepan of simmering water, and heat until melted. Stir until smooth, then leave at room temperature until the chocolate is thick enough to spread.

4 Split the cake horizontally in half. Use some of the chocolate mixture to sandwich the two halves together. Spread and decorate the top of the cake with the remaining chocolate mixture. Finally, whip the cream until soft peaks form and use to spread around the sides of the cake. Chill in the refrigerator until required. Serve cut into slices. Store in the refrigerator.

TASTY TIP

If buttermilk is unavailable, measure ¹/₄ cup of whole milk and add 2 teaspoons of lemon juice or white wine vinegar. Allow to stand for 1 hour at room temperature and then use as above.

1

2

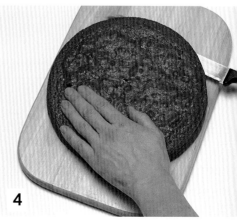

4

Peach & White Chocolate Cake

INGREDIENTS

Cuts into 8–10 slices

3/4 cup (1½ sticks) unsalted
butter, softened

2 tsp. grated orange zest

3/4 cup superfine sugar

3 large eggs

3½ oz white chocolate,
melted and cooled

2 cups self-rising flour, sifted

1 cup heavy cream

⅓ cup confectioners' sugar

1 cup toasted and chopped hazelnuts

For the peach filling:

2 peeled and chopped ripe peaches

2 tbsp. peach or orange liqueur

1 cup heavy cream

⅓ cup confectioners' sugar

1 Preheat the oven to 325°F. Lightly grease and line a deep 9-inch round cake pan. Cream the butter, orange zest, and sugar together until light and fluffy. Add the eggs, one at a time, beating well after each addition, then beat in the cooled white chocolate.

2 Add the flour and ¾ cup of water in two batches. Spoon into the prepared pan and bake in the preheated oven for 1½ hours or until firm. Allow to stand for at least 5 minutes before turning out onto a wire rack to cool completely.

3 To make the filling, place the peaches in a bowl and pour over the liqueur. Allow to stand for 30 minutes. Whip the cream with the confectioners' sugar until soft peaks form, then fold in peach mixture.

4 Split the cooled cake into three layers, place one layer on a serving plate, and spread with half the peach filling. Top with a second sponge layer and spread with the remaining peach filling. Top with remaining cake.

5 Whip the cream and confectioners' sugar together until soft peaks form. Spread over the top and sides of the cake, piping some onto the top if desired. Press hazelnuts into the side of the cake and, if desired, sprinkle a few on top. Serve cut into slices. Store in refrigerator.

TASTY TIP

When fresh peaches are out of season, use drained and chopped canned peaches instead.

1

2

3

Dark Chocolate Layered Torte

INGREDIENTS

Cuts into 10–12 slices

³/₄ cup (1¹/₂ sticks) butter

1 tbsp. instant coffee grounds

5 oz. semisweet dark chocolate

1¹/₂ cups superfine sugar

1¹/₄ cups self-rising flour

1 cup all-purpose flour

2 tbsp. unsweetened cocoa

2 large eggs

1 tsp. vanilla extract

7¹/₂ oz. semisweet dark
  chocolate, melted

¹/₂ cup (1 stick) butter, melted

¹/₃ cup confectioners' sugar, sifted

2 tsp. raspberry jelly

2¹/₂ tbsp. chocolate liqueur

³/₄ cup toasted slivered almonds

TASTY TIP

For the best flavor, use dark chocolate that has 70 percent cocoa solids.

1 Preheat the oven to 300°F. Lightly grease and line a 9-inch square cake pan. Melt the butter in a saucepan, remove from the heat, and stir in the coffee granules and 1 cup hot water. Add the semisweet dark chocolate and sugar, and stir until smooth, then pour into a bowl.

2 In another bowl, sift together the flours and unsweetened cocoa. Using an electric mixer, beat the sifted mixture into the chocolate mixture until smooth. Beat in the eggs and vanilla extract. Pour into the pan and bake in the preheated oven for 1¹/₄ hours or until firm. Leave for at least 5 minutes before turning out onto a wire rack to cool.

3 Meanwhile, mix together 7 oz. of the melted semisweet dark chocolate with the butter and confectioners' sugar, and beat until smooth. Let cool, then beat again. Set aside 4–5 tablespoons of the chocolate filling.

4 Cut the cooled cake in half to make two rectangles, then split each rectangle in three horizontally. Place one cake layer on a serving plate and spread thinly with the jelly, and then a thin layer of dark chocolate filling. Top with a second cake layer and sprinkle with a little liqueur, then spread thinly with filling. Repeat with remaining cake layers, liqueur, and filling.

5 Chill in the refrigerator for 2–3 hours or until firm. Cover the cake with the chocolate filling and press the slivered almonds into the sides of the cake. Place the remaining melted chocolate in a nonstick parchment paper decorating bag. Snip a small hole in the tip and pipe thin lines, ³/₄ inch apart, crosswise over the cake. Drag a toothpick lengthwise through the frosting in alternating directions to create a feathered effect. Serve.

3

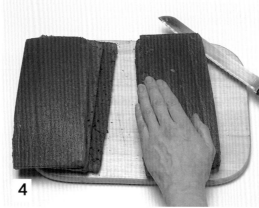

4

6

Chocolate Mousse Sponge

INGREDIENTS

Cuts into 8–10 slices

3 large eggs
⅓ cup sugar
1 tsp. vanilla extract
½ cup self-rising flour, sifted
¼ cup ground almonds
2 oz. semisweet dark
  chocolate, grated
confectioners' sugar, for dusting
freshly sliced strawberries,
  to decorate

For the mousse:

2 sheets gelatin
¼ cup heavy cream
3½ oz. semisweet dark
  chocolate, chopped
1 tsp. vanilla extract
4 large egg whites
½ cup sugar

TASTY TIP

Sheet gelatin is very easy to use. Soak the gelatin as described in step 2, then squeeze out the excess liquid. It must be added to hot liquid, where it will melt on contact.

1　Preheat the oven to 350°F. Lightly grease and line a 9-inch round cake pan, and lightly grease the sides of a 9-inch springform pan. Beat the eggs, sugar, and vanilla extract until thick and creamy. Fold in the flour, ground almonds, and semisweet dark chocolate. Spoon the batter into the prepared round cake pan and bake in the preheated oven for 25 minutes or until firm. Turn out onto a wire rack to cool.

2　For the mousse, soak the gelatin in ¼ cup of cold water for 5 minutes until softened. Meanwhile, heat the heavy cream in a small saucepan. when almost boiling, remove from the heat and stir in the chocolate and vanilla extract. Stir until the chocolate melts. Squeeze the excess water out of the gelatin and add to the chocolate mixture. Stir until dissolved, then pour into a large bowl.

3　Beat the egg whites until stiff, then gradually add the sugar, beating well between each addition. Fold the egg white mixture into the chocolate mixture in two batches.

4　Split the cake into two layers. Place one layer in the bottom of the springform pan. Pour in the chocolate mousse mixture, then top with the second layer of cake. Chill in the refrigerator for 4 hours or until the mousse has set. Loosen the sides and remove the cake from the pan. Dust with confectioners' sugar and decorate the top with a few freshly sliced strawberries. Serve cut into slices

1

3

4

Chocolate Chiffon Cake

INGREDIENTS

Cuts into 10–12 slices

¹/₂ cup unsweetened cocoa

2³/₄ cups self-rising flour

2¹/₂ cups sugar

7 large eggs, separated

¹/₄ cup vegetable oil

1 tsp. vanilla extract

³/₄ cup walnuts

7 oz. semisweet dark
  chocolate, melted

For the frosting:

³/₄ cups (1¹/₂ sticks) butter

2¹/₂ cups confectioners' sugar, sifted

2 tbsp. unsweetened cocoa, sifted

2 tbsp. brandy

1 Preheat the oven to 325°F. Lightly grease and line a 9-inch round cake pan. Lightly grease a baking pan. Blend the unsweetened cocoa with ³/₄ cup of boiling water, and let cool. Place the flour and 1¹/₂ cups of the sugar in a large bowl, and add the cocoa mixture, egg yolks, oil, and vanilla extract. Beat until smooth and lighter in color.

2 Beat the egg whites in a clean, grease-free bowl until soft peaks form, then fold into the cocoa mixture. Pour into the prepared pan and bake in the preheated oven for 1 hour or until firm. Leave for 5 minutes before turning out onto a wire rack to cool.

3 To make the frosting, cream together 1 stick of the butter with the confectioners' sugar, unsweetened cocoa, and brandy until smooth, then set aside. Melt the remaining butter and blend with about two-thirds of the melted semisweet dark chocolate. Stir until smooth and then leave until thickened.

4 Place the remaining sugar into a small, heavy saucepan over a low heat and heat until the sugar has melted and is a deep golden brown.

5 Add the walnuts and the remaining melted chocolate to the melted sugar and pour onto the prepared baking pan. Leave until cold and brittle, then chop finely. Set aside.

6 Split the cake into three layers, place one layer onto a large serving plate, and spread with half of the brandy butter frosting. Top with a second cake layer, spread with the remaining brandy butter frosting, and arrange the third cake layer on top. Cover the cake with the thickened chocolate glaze. Sprinkle with the walnut praline and serve.

HELPFUL HINT

Do not overmix the batter in step 2 or the cake will be heavy instead of very light and spongy.

2

6

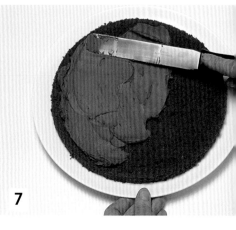

7

Sachertorte

INGREDIENTS

Cuts into 10–12 slices

5 oz. semisweet dark chocolate
²/₃ cup (1¼ sticks) unsalted
   butter, softened
½ cup superfine sugar, plus 2 tbsp.
3 large eggs, separated
1¼ cups all-purpose flour, sifted

To decorate:

²/₃ cup apricot jelly
4 oz. semisweet dark
   chocolate, chopped
½ cup (1 stick) unsalted butter
1 oz. milk chocolate

FOOD FACT

In 1832, the Viennese foreign minister asked a Vienna hotel to prepare an especially tempting cake. The head pastry chef was ill and so the task fell to second-year apprentice, Franz Sacher, who presented this delightful cake.

1 Preheat the oven to 350°F. Lightly grease and line a deep 9-inch cake pan.

2 Melt the 5 oz. of semisweet dark chocolate in a heatproof bowl set over a saucepan of simmering water. Stir in 1 tablespoon of water and allow to cool.

3 Beat the butter and ½ cup of the sugar together until light and fluffy. Beat in the egg yolks, one at a time, beating well between each addition. Stir in the melted chocolate, then the flour.

4 In a clean, grease-free bowl, beat the egg whites until stiff peaks form, then beat in the remaining sugar. Fold into the chocolate mixture and spoon into the prepared pan. Bake in the preheated oven for 30 minutes or until firm. Leave for 5 minutes, then turn out onto a wire rack to cool. Leave the cake upside down.

5 To decorate the cake, split the cold cake in two and place one half on a serving plate. Heat the jelly and rub through a fine strainer. Brush half the jelly onto the first cake half, then cover with the remaining cake layer and brush with the remaining jelly. Leave for 1 hour or until the jelly has set.

6 Place the semisweet dark chocolate and the butter into a heatproof bowl set over a saucepan of simmering water, and heat until the chocolate has melted. Stir occasionally until smooth, then leave until thickened. Use to cover the cake.

7 Melt the milk chocolate in a heatproof bowl set over a saucepan of simmering water. Place in a small wax paper decorating bag and snip a small hole at the tip. Pipe "Sacher" with a large "S" on the top. Allow to set at room temperature.

3

4

5

Chocolate Roulade

INGREDIENTS

Cuts into 8 slices

7 oz. semisweet dark chocolate
1 cup superfine sugar
7 large eggs, separated
1 cup heavy cream
3 tbsp. Cointreau or Grand Marnier
4 tbsp. confectioners' sugar,
  for dusting

To decorate:
fresh raspberries
sprigs of fresh mint

TASTY TIP

Leaving the cake in the pan overnight gives it a fudgy texture and also means that the cake is less likely to break when it is rolled up.

1 Preheat the oven to 350°F. Lightly grease and line a 9 inch x 13-inch jelly-roll pan with nonstick parchment paper.

2 Break the chocolate into small pieces into a heatproof bowl set over a saucepan of simmering water. Leave until almost melted, stirring occasionally. Remove from the heat and let stand for 5 minutes.

3 Beat the egg yolks with the sugar until pale and creamy and the whisk leaves a trail in the mixture when lifted. Carefully fold in the melted chocolate.

4 In a clean, grease-free bowl, beat the egg whites until stiff, then fold one large spoonful into the chocolate mixture.

5 Mix lightly, then gently fold in the remaining egg whites. Pour the batter into the prepared pan and level the surface. Bake in the preheated oven for 20–25 minutes or until firm.

6 Remove the cake from the oven, leave in the pan, and cover with a wire rack and a damp dish towel. Leave for 8 hours or preferably overnight.

7 Dust a large sheet of nonstick parchment paper generously with 2 tablespoons of the confectioners' sugar. Unwrap the cake and turn out onto the wax paper. Remove the parchment paper.

8 Whip the cream with the liqueur until soft peaks form. Spread over the cake, leaving a 1-inch border all around.

9 Using the paper to help, roll the cake up from a short end. Transfer to a serving plate, seam-side down, and dust with the remaining confectioners' sugar. Decorate with fresh raspberries and mint. Serve.

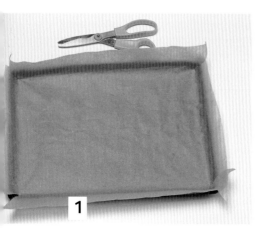

1

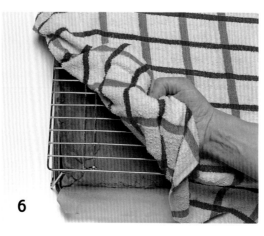

6

9

Supreme Chocolate Cake

INGREDIENTS

Cuts into 10–12 slices

For the cake:
1½ cups self-rising flour, sifted
1½ tsp. baking powder, sifted
3 tbsp. unsweetened cocoa, sifted
¾ cup (1½ sticks) butter, softened
¾ cup superfine sugar
3 extra-large eggs

To decorate:
12 oz. semisweet dark chocolate
1 gelatin leaf
1 cup heavy cream
6 tbsp. butter
unsweetened cocoa, for dusting

HELPFUL HINT
If you prefer, make ordinary chocolate curls to decorate this cake.

1 Preheat the oven to 350°F. Lightly grease and line three 8-inch round cake pans. Place all the cake ingredients into a bowl and beat together until thick. Add a little warm water if too thick. Divide the batter evenly among the prepared pans. Bake in the preheated oven for 35–40 minutes until a toothpick inserted in the center comes out clean. Cool on wire racks.

2 Very gently, heat 2 tablespoons of hot water with 2 oz. of the chocolate, and stir until combined. Remove from the heat and leave for 5 minutes. Place the gelatin into a shallow dish and add 2 tablespoons cold water. Leave for 5 minutes, then squeeze out any excess water and add to the chocolate and water mixture. Stir until dissolved. Whip the heavy cream until just thickened. Add the chocolate mixture and continue beating until soft peaks form. Leave until starting to set.

3 Place one of the cakes onto a serving plate and spread with half the cream mixture. Top with a second cake and the remaining cream, cover with the third cake, and chill in the refrigerator until set.

4 Melt half the remaining chocolate with the butter, and stir until smooth. Allow to thicken. Melt the remaining chocolate. Cut 12 4-inch squares of foil. Spread the chocolate evenly over the squares to within 1 inch of the edges. Refrigerate for 3–4 minutes until just set but not brittle. Gather up the corners and crimp together. Return to the refrigerator until firm.

5 Spread the chocolate and butter mixture over the top and sides of the cake. Remove the foil from the giant curls and use to decorate the top of the cake. Dust with unsweetened cocoa and serve cut into wedges.

1

2

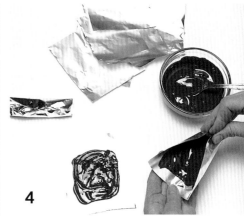

4

Black Forest Cake

INGREDIENTS

Cuts into 10–12 slices

1 cup plus 2 tbsp (2¼ sticks) butter

1 tbsp. instant coffee grounds

1½ cups hot water

7 oz. semisweet dark chocolate, chopped or broken

1¾ cups superfine sugar

2 cups self-rising flour

1¼ cups all-purpose flour

½ cup unsweetened cocoa

2 large eggs

2 tsp. vanilla extract

2 14-oz. cans pitted cherries in juice

2 tsp. arrowroot

2 cups heavy cream

¼ cup kirsch

HELPFUL HINT

The cake can be assembled and served right away but will benefit from being refrigerated for 1–2 hours so the cream sets slightly. This will make slicing easier.

1 Preheat the oven to 300°F. Lightly grease and line a deep 9-inch cake pan.

2 Melt the butter in a large saucepan. Blend the coffee with the hot water, add to the butter with the chocolate and sugar, and heat gently, stirring until smooth. Pour into a large bowl and leave until just warm.

3 Sift together the flours and unsweetened cocoa. Using an electric mixer, beat the warm chocolate mixture on a low speed, then gradually beat in the dry ingredients. Beat in the eggs one at a time, then add the vanilla extract.

4 Pour the batter into the prepared pan and bake in the preheated oven for 1 hour and 45 minutes or until firm and a toothpick inserted into the center comes out clean. Leave the cake in the pan for 5 minutes to cool slightly before turning out onto a wire rack.

5 Place the cherries and their juice in a small saucepan and heat gently. Blend the arrowroot with 2 teaspoons of water until smooth, then stir into the cherries. Cook, stirring until the liquid thickens. Simmer very gently for 2 minutes, then leave until cooled.

6 Beat the heavy cream until thick. Trim the top of the cake if necessary, then split the cake into three layers. Brush the bottom of the cake with half the kirsch. Top with a layer of cream and one-third of the cherries. Repeat the layering, then place the third layer on top.

7 Set aside a little cream for decorating and use the remainder to cover the top and sides of the cake. Pipe a decorative edge around the cake, then arrange the remaining cherries in the center and serve.

3

5

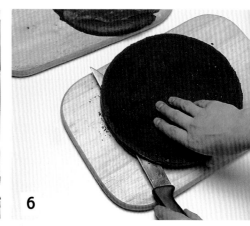

6

Whole Orange & Chocolate Cake with Marmalade Cream

INGREDIENTS

Cuts into 6–8 slices

1 small scrubbed orange

2 large eggs, separated , plus
 1 whole egg

1¼ cups superfine sugar

1 cup ground almonds

3 oz. semisweet dark
 chocolate, melted

½ cup heavy cream

¾ cup cream cheese

¼ cup confectioners' sugar

2 tbsp. orange marmalade

orange zest, to decorate

HELPFUL HINT

This cake contains no flour and is therefore likely to sink in the center on cooling. This is normal and does not mean that the cake is not cooked.

1 Preheat the oven to 350°F. Lightly grease and line the bottom of a loaf pan. Place the orange in a small saucepan, cover with cold water, and bring to a boil. Simmer for 1 hour or until completely soft. Drain and let cool.

2 Place 2 egg yolks, 1 whole egg, and the sugar in a heatproof bowl set over a saucepan of simmering water, and beat until doubled in bulk. Remove from the heat and continue to beat for 5 minutes until cooled.

3 Cut the whole orange in half and discard the seeds, then place in a food processor or blender and blend to a purée.

4 Carefully fold the purée into the egg yolk mixture with the ground almonds and melted chocolate.

5 Beat the egg whites until stiff peaks form. Fold a large spoonful of the egg whites into the chocolate mixture, then gently fold the remaining egg whites into the mixture. Pour into the prepared pan and bake in the preheated oven for 50 minutes or until firm and a toothpick inserted into the center comes out clean. Cool in the pan before turning out of the pan and carefully discarding the lining paper.

6 Meanwhile, whip the heavy cream until just thickened. In another bowl, blend the cream cheese with the confectioners' sugar and marmalade until smooth, then fold in the heavy cream. Chill the marmalade cream in the refrigerator until needed. Decorate with orange zest, cut in slices, and serve with the marmalade cream.

2

4

6

White Chocolate & Raspberry Mousse Cake

INGREDIENTS

Cuts into 8 slices

4 large eggs

$^1/_2$ cup superfine sugar

$^3/_4$ cup all-purpose flour, sifted

$^1/_4$ cup cornstarch, sifted

3 gelatin leaves

4 cups raspberries, thawed if frozen

14 oz. white chocolate

$^3/_4$ cup fromage frais or reduced-fat sour cream

2 large egg whites

2 tbsp. superfine sugar

4 tbsp. raspberry or orange liqueur

$^3/_4$ cup heavy cream

fresh raspberries, halved, to decorate

HELPFUL HINT

Don't try to wrap the chocolate-covered parchment around the cake before it's set, or it will run and be uneven.

1 Preheat the oven to 375°F. Grease and line two 9-inch cake pans. Beat the eggs and sugar until thick and creamy and the whisk leaves a trail in the mixture. Fold in the flour and cornstarch, then divide among the pans. Bake in the preheated oven for 12–15 minutes or until risen and firm. Cool in the pans, then turn out onto wire racks.

2 Place the gelatin with 4 tablespoons of cold water in a dish and let soften for 5 minutes. Purée half the raspberries, press through a strainer, then heat until nearly boiling. Squeeze out excess water from the gelatin, add to the purée, and stir until dissolved. Set aside.

3 Melt 6 oz. of the chocolate in a bowl set over a saucepan of simmering water. Let cool, then stir in the yogurt and purée. Beat the egg whites until stiff and beat in the sugar. Fold into the raspberry mixture with the rest of the raspberries.

4 Line the sides of a 9-inch springform pan with nonstick parchment paper. Place one layer of sponge in the bottom and sprinkle with half the liqueur. Pour in the raspberry mixture and top with the second sponge. Brush with the remaining liqueur. Press down and chill in the refrigerator for 4 hours. Unmold onto a plate.

5 Cut a strip of double-thick nonstick parchment paper to fit around the cake and stand $^1/_2$ inch higher. Melt the remaining white chocolate and spread thickly onto the paper. Leave until just setting. Wrap around the cake and freeze for 15 minutes. Peel away the paper. Whip the cream until thick and spread over the top. Decorate with raspberries.

1

2

4

Chocolate Orange Fudge Cake

INGREDIENTS

Cuts into 8–10 slices

$^2/_3$ cup unsweetened cocoa

1 tbsp. grated orange zest

3 cups self-rising flour

2 tsp. baking powder

1 tsp. baking soda

$^1/_2$ tsp. salt

1 cup firmly packed golden
  brown sugar

$3^1/_4$ cup ($1^1/_2$ sticks) butter, softened

3 large eggs

1 tsp. vanilla extract

$1^1/_8$ cup sour cream

6 tbsp. butter

6 tbsp. milk

thinly pared zest of 1 orange

6 tbsp. unsweetened cocoa

$2^1/_4$ cups confectioners' sugar, sifted

1 Preheat the oven to 350°F. Lightly grease and line two 9-inch round cake pans with nonstick parchment paper. Blend the unsweetened cocoa and $^1/_4$ cup of boiling water until smooth. Stir in the orange zest and set aside. Sift together the flour, baking powder, baking soda, and salt, then set aside. Cream together the sugar and softened butter, and beat in the eggs, one at a time, then the cocoa mixture and vanilla extract. Finally, stir in the flour mixture and the sour cream in alternating spoonfuls.

2 Divide the batter among the prepared pans and bake in the preheated oven for 35 minutes or until the edges of the cake pull away from the pan and the tops spring back when lightly pressed. Cool in the pans for 10 minutes, then turn out onto wire racks until cold.

3 Gently heat the butter and milk with the pared orange zest. Simmer for 10 minutes, stirring occasionally. Remove from the heat and discard the orange zest.

4 Pour the warm orange and milk mixture into a large bowl and stir in the unsweetened cocoa. Gradually beat in the sifted confectioners' sugar and beat until the frosting is smooth and spreadable. Place one cake onto a large serving plate. Top with about one-quarter of the frosting, place the second cake on top, then cover the cake with the remaining frosting. Serve.

HELPFUL HINT

This cake keeps exceptionally well in an airtight container for up to five days.

1

2

4

Cranberry & White Chocolate Cake

INGREDIENTS

Cuts into 4–6 slices

1 cup (2 sticks) butter, softened

1⅛ cup cream cheese

⅔ cup firmly packed golden brown sugar

1 cup superfine sugar

3 tsp. grated orange zest

1 tsp. vanilla extract

4 large eggs

3¼ cups all-purpose flour

2 tsp. baking powder

¾ cup cranberries, thawed if frozen

8 oz. white chocolate, coarsely chopped

2 tbsp. orange juice

1 Preheat the oven to 350°F. Lightly grease and flour a 9-inch fancy tube mold (kugelhopf pan) or ring mold. Using an electric mixer, cream the butter and cheese with the sugars until light and fluffy. Add the grated orange zest and vanilla extract, and beat until smooth. Beat in the eggs, one at a time.

2 Sift the flour and baking powder together, and stir into the creamed batter, beating well after each addition. Fold in the cranberries and 6 oz. of the white chocolate. Spoon into the prepared mold and bake in the preheated oven for 1 hour or until firm and a toothpick inserted into the center comes out clean. Cool in the mold before turning out onto on a wire rack.

3 Melt the remaining white chocolate, stir until smooth, then stir in the orange juice and let cool until thickened. Transfer the cake to a serving plate and spoon over the white chocolate and orange glaze. Allow to set.

TASTY TIP

If cranberries are not available, substitute chopped dried apples, raisins, dried cranberries, or chopped dried apricots.

1

2

3

Fresh Strawberry Sponge Cake

INGREDIENTS

Cuts into 8–10 slices

$^3/_4$ cup (1$^1/_2$ sticks) unsalted
   butter, softened

$^3/_4$ cup superfine sugar

1 tsp. vanilla extract

3 extra-large beaten eggs

1 $^1/_2$ cups self-rising flour

$^1/_2$ cup heavy cream

2 tbsp. confectioners' sugar, sifted

1$^1/_2$ cups hulled and chopped
   fresh strawberries

extra strawberries, to decorate

HELPFUL HINT

For sponge cakes, it is important to achieve the correct consistency of the uncooked mixture. Check after folding in the flour by tapping a spoonful of the mixture on the side of the bowl. If it drops easily, "dropping" consistency has been reached. If it is stiff, add a tablespoon of cooled boiled water.

1   Preheat the oven to 375°F. Lightly grease and line the bases of two 8-inch round cake pans with wax paper or parchment paper.

2   Using an electric mixer, beat the butter, sugar, and vanilla extract until pale and fluffy. Gradually beat in the eggs, a little at a time, beating well between each addition.

3   Sift half the flour over the mixture, and using a metal spoon, gently fold into the mixture. Sift over the remaining flour and fold in until just blended.

4   Divide the mixture between the pans, spreading evenly. Gently smooth the surfaces with the back of a spoon. Bake in the center of the preheated oven for 20–25 minutes or until well risen and golden.

5   Remove and let cool before turning out onto a wire rack. Whip the cream with 1 tablespoon of the confectioners' sugar until it forms soft peaks. Fold in the chopped strawberries.

6   Spread the first cake layer evenly with the mixture and top with the second cake layer, rounded-side up.

7   Dust the cake with confectioners' sugar and decorate with the remaining berries. Slide onto a serving plate, and serve.

2

4

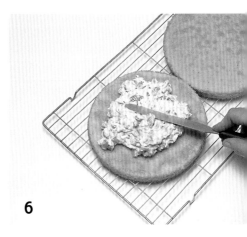

6

Almond Angel Cake with Amaretto Cream

INGREDIENTS

Cuts into 10–12 slices

1½ cups confectioners' sugar, plus
   2–3 tbsp.
1½ cups all-purpose flour
1½ cups egg whites (about 10
   extra-large egg whites)
1½ tsp. cream of tartar
½ tsp. vanilla extract
1 tsp. almond extract
¼ tsp. salt
1 scant cup superfine sugar
¾ cup heavy cream
2 tablespoons Amaretto liqueur
fresh raspberries, to decorate

FOOD FACT

Angel food cake has a very light and delicate texture, and can be difficult to slice. For best results, use 2 forks to gently separate a portion of the cake.

1 — Preheat the oven to 350°F. Sift together the 1½ cups confectioners' sugar and flour. Stir to blend, then sift again.

2 — Using an electric mixer, beat the egg whites, cream of tartar, vanilla extract, ½ teaspoon of almond extract, and salt on medium speed until soft peaks form. Gradually add the superfine sugar, 2 tablespoons at a time, beating well after each addition until stiff peaks form.

3 — Sift about one-third of the flour mixture over the egg-white mixture, and, using a metal spoon or rubber spatula, gently fold into the egg white mixture. Repeat, folding the flour mixture into the egg white mixture in two more batches. Spoon into an ungreased angel food cake pan or 10-inch tube pan.

4 — Bake in the preheated oven until risen and golden on top and the surface springs back quickly when gently pressed. Immediately invert the cake pan and cool completely in the pan. When cool, run a sharp knife around the edge and the center ring to loosen the cake from the edge. Using the fingertips, ease the cake from the pan and invert onto a cake plate. Thickly dust the cake with the extra confectioners' sugar.

5 — Whip the cream with the remaining almond extract, Amaretto liqueur, and a little more confectioners' sugar until soft peaks form.

6 — Fill a piping bag fitted with a star tip with half the cream, and pipe around the bottom of the cake. Decorate the edge with the fresh raspberries, and serve the remaining cream separately.

1

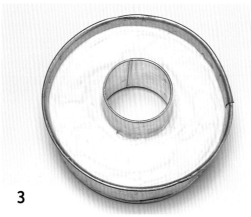

3

7

White Chocolate Cheesecake

INGREDIENTS

Cuts into 16 slices

For the base:
5 Graham crackers
½ cup lightly toasted whole almonds
4 tbsp. butter, melted
½ tsp. almond extract

For the filling:
12 oz. good-quality white
  chocolate, chopped
⅓ cup heavy cream
1½ lb. cream cheese, softened
4 tbsp. superfine sugar
4 extra-large eggs
2 tbsp. Amaretto or
  almond-flavor liqueur

For the topping:
2 cups sour cream
4 tbsp. superfine sugar
½ tsp. almond or vanilla extract
white chocolate curls, to decorate

1   Preheat the oven to 350°F. Lightly grease a 9-inch round springform pan. Crush the graham crackers and almonds in a food processor to form fine crumbs. Pour in the butter and almond extract, and blend. Pour the crumbs into the pan, and using the back of a spoon, press onto the bottom and up the sides to within ½ inch of the top of the pan edge.

2   Bake in the preheated oven for 5 minutes to set. Remove, and transfer to a wire rack. Reduce the oven temperature to 300°F.

3   Heat the white chocolate and cream in a saucepan over a low heat, stirring constantly until melted. Remove and cool.

4   Beat the cream cheese and sugar until smooth. Add the eggs, one at a time, beating well after each addition. Slowly beat in the cooled white chocolate cream and the Amaretto, and pour into the baked crust. Place on a cookie sheet, and bake for 45–55 minutes until the edge of the cake is firm, but the center is slightly soft. Reduce the oven temperature if the top begins to brown. Transfer to a wire rack and increase the temperature to 400°F.

5   To make the topping, beat the sour cream, sugar, and almond or vanilla extract until smooth, and gently pour over the cheesecake, tilting the pan to distribute the topping evenly. Alternatively, spread with a metal spatula.

6   Bake for another 5 minutes to set. Turn off the oven and leave the door halfway open for about 1 hour. Transfer to a wire rack, and run a sharp knife around the edge of the crust to separate from the pan. Cool and refrigerate until chilled. Remove from the pan, decorate with white chocolate curls, and serve.

1

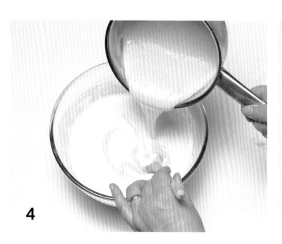

4

5

Italian Polenta Cake with Mascarpone Cream

INGREDIENTS

Cuts into 6–8 slices

1 tsp. butter and flour for the pan
1 scant cup all-purpose flour
¼ cup polenta or yellow cornmeal
1 tsp. baking powder
¼ tsp. salt
grated zest of 1 lemon
2 extra-large eggs
½ cup plus 2 tbsp.
 superfine sugar
5 tbsp. milk
½ tsp. almond extract
2 tbsp. seedless raisins or
 golden raisins
6 tbsp. unsalted butter, softened
2 medium dessert pears, peeled,
 cored, and thinly sliced
2 tbsp. apricot jelly
6 oz. mascarpone cheese
1–2 tsp. sugar
¼ cup heavy cream
2 tbsp. Amaretto liqueur or rum
2–3 tbsp. toasted, slivered almonds
confectioners' sugar, to dust

1 Preheat the oven to 375°F. Butter a 9-inch springform pan. Dust lightly with flour.

2 Stir the flour, polenta or cornmeal, baking powder, salt, and lemon zest together. Beat the eggs and half the sugar until light and fluffy. Slowly beat in the milk and almond extract.

3 Stir in the seedless or golden raisins, then beat in the flour mixture and 4 tablespoons of the butter.

4 Spoon into the pan and smooth the top evenly. Arrange the pear slices on top in overlapping concentric circles.

5 Melt the remaining butter and brush over the pear slices. Sprinkle with the rest of the sugar.

6 Bake in the preheated oven for about 40 minutes until puffed and golden, and the edges of the pears are lightly caramelized. Transfer to a wire rack. Set aside to cool in the pan for 15 minutes.

7 Remove the cake from the pan. Heat the apricot jelly with 1 tablespoon water and brush over the top of the cake to glaze.

8 Beat the mascarpone cheese with the sugar, the cream, and Amaretto or rum until smooth and forming a soft, dropping consistency.

9 When cool, sprinkle the almonds over the polenta cake and dust generously with the confectioners' sugar. Serve the cake with the liqueur-flavored mascarpone cream separately or on the side.

1

4

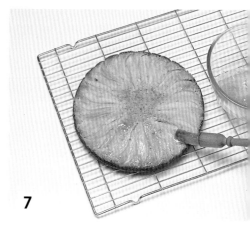

7

Fall Apple Cake

INGREDIENTS

Cuts into 8–10 slices

2 cups self-rising flour

1¹/₂ tsp. baking powder

²/₃ cup (1¹/₄ cups) margarine, softened

¹/₂ cup plus 2 tbsp. superfine sugar,
   plus extra for sprinkling

1 tsp. vanilla extract

2 large beaten eggs

2¹/₂ lb. apples, peeled, cored,
   and sliced

1 tbsp. lemon juice

¹/₂ tsp. ground cinnamon

fresh custard sauce or cream,
   to serve

1 Preheat the oven to 325°F. Lightly grease and line the base of an 8-inch cake pan with nonstick parchment paper or wax paper. Sift the flour and baking powder into a small bowl.

2 Beat the margarine, sugar, and vanilla extract until light and fluffy. Gradually beat in the eggs, a little at a time, beating well after each addition. Stir in the flour.

3 Spoon about one third of the mixture into the pan, smoothing the surface. Toss the apple slices in the lemon juice and cinnamon, and spoon over the cake mixture, making a thick, even layer. Spread the remaining mixture over the apple layer to the edge of the pan, making sure the apples are covered. Smooth the top with the back of a wet spoon, and sprinkle generously with sugar.

4 Bake in the preheated oven for 1¹/₂ hours or until well risen and golden, the apples are tender, and the center of the cake springs back when pressed lightly. If the top browns too quickly, reduce the oven temperature slightly and cover the cake loosely with foil.

5 Transfer to a wire rack and cool for about 20 minutes in the pan. Run a thin knife blade between the cake and the pan to loosen the cake, and invert onto a paper-lined rack. Turn the cake right-side up, and cool. Serve with the custard sauce or cream.

FOOD FACT

Cooking apples are extremely versatile, as they can be baked, puréed, poached, and used in cakes and pies, as well as savory foods. Apples have a good soluble fiber content, making them an extremely nutritious food.

3

3

5

Thanksgiving Cranberry Chocolate Roulade

INGREDIENTS

Cuts into 12–14 slices

For the chocolate ganache frosting:
1¼ cups heavy cream
12 oz. semisweet dark
    chocolate, chopped
2 tbsp. brandy (optional)

For the roulade:
5 extra-large eggs, separated
3 tbsp. unsweetened cocoa, sifted,
    plus extra for dusting
1 cup confectioners' sugar, sifted,
    plus extra for dusting
¼ tsp. cream of tartar

For the filling:
¾ cup cranberry sauce
1–2 tbsp. brandy (optional)
⅔ cup heavy cream, whipped to
    soft peaks

To decorate:
candied orange strips
dried cranberries

1 Preheat the oven to 400°F. Bring the cream to a boil over medium heat. Remove from the heat and add all of the chocolate, stirring until melted. Stir in the brandy, if desired, and strain into a medium bowl. Cool, then refrigerate for 6–8 hours.

2 Lightly grease and line a 10 x 15-inch jelly-roll pan with nonstick parchment paper. Using an electric mixer, beat the egg yolks until thick and creamy. Slowly beat in the cocoa and half the confectioners' sugar, and set aside. Beat the egg whites and tartar into soft peaks. Gradually beat in the remaining sugar until the mixture is stiff and glossy. Gently fold the yolk mixture into the egg whites with a metal spoon or rubber spatula. Spread evenly into the pan.

3 Bake in the preheated oven for 15 minutes. Remove, then invert onto a large sheet of wax paper dusted with cocoa. Cut off the crisp edges of the cake, then roll up. Leave on a wire rack until cool.

4 For the filling, heat the cranberry sauce with the brandy, if desired, until warm and spreadable. Unroll the cooled cake and spread with the cranberry sauce. Allow to cool and set. Carefully spoon the whipped cream over the surface and spread to within 1 inch of the edges. Roll the cake again. Transfer to a cake plate or tray.

5 Allow the chocolate ganache to soften at room temperature, then beat until soft and of a spreadable consistency. Spread over the roulade, and using a fork, mark the roulade with ridges to resemble tree bark. Dust with confectioners' sugar. Decorate with the candied orange strips and dried cranberries, and serve.

3

4

5

Buttery Passion Fruit Madeira Cake

INGREDIENTS

Cuts into 8–10 slices

2 scant cups all-purpose flour

1 tsp. baking powder

$^3/_4$ cup ($1^1/_2$ sticks) unsalted
   butter, softened

1 cup plus 2 tbsp. superfine sugar,
   plus 1 tsp. for sprinkling

grated zest of 1 orange

1 tsp. vanilla extract

3 large eggs, beaten

2 tbsp. milk

6 ripe passion fruit

5 tbsp. confectioners' sugar

confectioners' sugar, to dust

FOOD FACT

Regardless of its name, Madeira cake does not actually originate from the Portuguese-owned island of Madeira. It is, in fact, a traditional English cake that was often served with Madeira, a fortified wine which does derive its name from the island.

1 Preheat the oven to 350°F. Lightly grease and line the base of a 5 x 9-inch loaf pan with wax paper. Sift the flour and baking powder into a bowl, and set aside.

2 Beat the butter, sugar, orange zest, and vanilla extract until light and fluffy, then gradually beat in the eggs, 1 tablespoon at a time, beating well after each addition. If the mixture appears to curdle or separate, beat in a little of the flour mixture.

3 Fold in the flour mixture with the milk until just blended. Do not overmix. Spoon lightly into the prepared pan and smooth the top evenly. Sprinkle lightly with the teaspoon of superfine sugar.

4 Bake in the preheated oven for 55 minutes or until well risen and golden brown. Remove and cool for 15–20 minutes. Turn the cake out of the pan and discard the lining paper.

5 Cut the passion fruit in half, and scoop out the pulp into a sieve set over a bowl. Press the juice through using a rubber spatula or wooden spoon. Stir in the confectioners' sugar and stir to dissolve, adding a little extra sugar if necessary.

6 Using a skewer, pierce holes all over the cake. Slowly spoon the passion fruit glaze over the cake and allow it to seep in. Gently invert the cake onto a wire rack, then turn it right-side up. Dust with confectioners' sugar and cool completely. Serve cold.

3

5

6

Lemony Coconut Cake

INGREDIENTS

Cuts into 10–12 slices

2½ cups all-purpose flour

2 tbsp. cornstarch

1 tbsp. baking powder

1 tsp. salt

⅔ cup (1¼ sticks) shortening or
   soft margarine

1¼ cups superfine sugar

grated zest of 2 lemons

1 tsp. vanilla extract

3 extra-large eggs

⅔ cup milk

4 tbsp. Malibu or rum

16-oz. jar lemon curd (available from
   specialty grocery stores)

lime zest, to decorate

For the frosting:

1¼ cups superfine sugar

½ cup water

1 tbsp. glucose

¼ tsp. salt

1 tsp. vanilla extract

3 extra-large egg whites

½ cup unsweetened shredded
   dry coconut

1. Preheat the oven to 350°F. Lightly grease and flour two 8-inch, round, nonstick cake pans.

2. Sift the flour, cornstarch, baking powder, and salt into a large bowl, and add the shortening or margarine, sugar, lemon zest, vanilla extract, eggs, and milk. With an electric mixer on a low speed, beat until blended, adding a little extra milk if the mixture is very stiff. Increase the speed to medium and beat for about 2 minutes.

3. Divide the mixture between the pans and smooth the tops evenly. Bake in the preheated oven for 20–25 minutes or until the cakes feel firm and are cooked. Remove from the oven, and cool before removing from the pans.

4. Put all the ingredients for the frosting, except the coconut, into a heatproof bowl placed over a saucepan of simmering water. Do not allow the base of the bowl to touch the water.

5. Using an electric mixer, blend the frosting ingredients on a low speed. Increase the speed to high, and beat for 7 minutes until the whites are stiff and glossy. Remove the bowl from the heat and continue beating until cool. Cover with plastic wrap.

6. Using a serrated knife, split the cake layers horizontally in half and sprinkle each cut surface with the Malibu or rum. Sandwich the cakes together with the lemon curd, and press lightly.

7. Spread the top and sides generously with the frosting, swirling the top. Sprinkle the coconut over the top and gently press onto the sides to cover. Decorate the coconut cake with the lime zest, and serve.

2

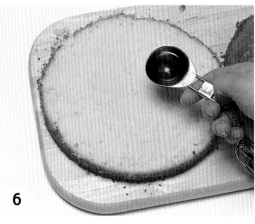

6

7

Wild Strawberry & Rose Petal Jelly Cake

INGREDIENTS

Cuts into 8 slices

2½ cups all-purpose flour
1 tsp. baking powder
¼ tsp. salt
⅔ cup (1¼ stick) unsalted
   butter, softened
1 scant cup superfine sugar
2 extra-large eggs, beaten
2 tbsp. rosewater
½ cup milk
½ cup rose petal or strawberry jelly,
   slightly warmed
¾ cup hulled wild strawberries, or
   chopped baby strawberries
frosted rose petals, to decorate

Rose cream filling:

¾ cup heavy cream
1 tbsp. Greek yogurt
2 tbsp. rosewater
1–2 tbsp. confectioners' sugar

1 Preheat the oven to 350°F. Lightly grease and flour an 8-inch, round, nonstick cake pan. Sift the flour, baking powder, and salt into a bowl, and set aside.

2 Beat the butter and sugar until light and fluffy. Beat in the eggs, a little at a time, then stir in the rosewater. Gently fold in the flour mixture and milk with a metal spoon or rubber spatula, and mix lightly together.

3 Spoon the cake mixture into the pan, spreading evenly and smoothing the top.

4 Bake in the preheated oven for 25–30 minutes or until well risen and golden, and the center springs back when pressed with a clean finger. Remove from the oven and cool, then remove from the pan.

5 For the filling, beat the cream, yogurt, 1 tablespoon of rosewater, and 1 tablespoon of confectioners' sugar until soft peaks form. Split the cake horizontally in half, and sprinkle with the remaining rosewater.

6 Spread the warmed jelly on the base. Top with half the whipped cream mixture, then sprinkle with half the strawberries. Place the remaining cake-half on top. Spread with the remaining cream and swirl, if desired. Decorate with the rose petals. Dust the cake lightly with a little confectioners' sugar, and serve.

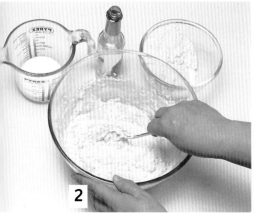
2

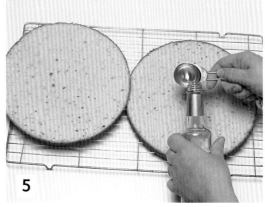
5

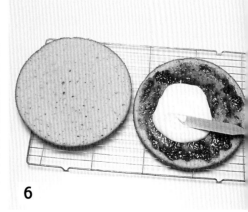
6

Raspberry & Hazelnut Meringue Cake

INGREDIENTS

Cuts into 8 slices

For the meringue:

4 extra-large egg whites

1/4 tsp. cream of tartar

1 cup superfine sugar

3/4 cup skinned, toasted, and finely ground hazelnuts

For the filling:

1 1/4 cups heavy cream

1 tbsp. confectioners' sugar

1–2 tbsp. raspberry-flavored liqueur (optional)

2 1/2 cups fresh raspberries

1 Preheat the oven to 275°F. Line two cookie sheets with nonstick parchment paper and draw an 8-inch circle on each. Beat the egg whites and cream of tartar until soft peaks form, then gradually beat in the sugar, 2 tablespoons at a time.

2 Beat well after each addition until the whites are stiff and glossy. Using a metal spoon or rubber spatula, gently fold in the ground hazelnuts.

3 Divide the mixture evenly between the two circles and spread neatly. Swirl one of the circles to make a decorative top layer. Bake in the preheated oven for about 1 1/2 hours until crisp and dry. Turn off the oven and allow the meringues to cool for 1 hour. Transfer to a wire rack to cool completely. Carefully peel off the papers.

4 For the filling, whip the cream, confectioners' sugar, and liqueur, if desired, together until soft peaks form. Place the flat round on a serving plate. Spread over most of the cream, setting aside some for decorating, and arrange the raspberries in concentric circles over the cream.

5 Place the swirly meringue on top of the cream and raspberries, pressing down gently. Pipe the remaining cream onto the meringue, decorate with a few raspberries, and serve.

HELPFUL HINT

It is essential when beating egg whites that the bowl being used is completely clean and dry, as any grease or oil will prevent egg whites from gaining volume needed.

2

3

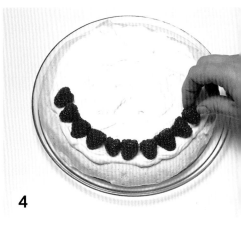

4

Chocolate & Almond Daquoise with Summer Berries

INGREDIENTS

Cuts into 8 slices

For the almond meringues:

6 extra-large egg whites

¼ tsp. cream of tartar

1 cup plus 4 tbsp. superfine sugar

½ tsp. almond extract

½ cup lightly toasted and finely ground blanched or slivered almonds

For the chocolate buttercream:

6 tbsp. butter, softened

4 cups confectioners' sugar, sifted

6 tbsp. unsweetened cocoa, sifted

3–4 tbsp. milk or light cream

3 cups mixed summer berries such as raspberries, strawberries, and blackberries

To decorate:

toasted slivered almonds

confectioners' sugar

1 Preheat the oven to 275°F. Line three cookie sheets with nonstick parchment paper and draw an 8-inch circle on each one.

2 Beat the egg whites and cream of tartar until soft peaks form. Gradually beat in the sugar, 2 tablespoons at a time, beating well after each addition until the whites are stiff and glossy.

3 Beat in the almond extract, then using a metal spoon or rubber spatula, gently fold in the ground almonds.

4 Divide the mixture evenly between the three circles of parchment paper, spreading neatly into the circles and smoothing the tops evenly.

5 Bake in the preheated oven for about 1¼ hours or until crisp, rotating the cookie sheets halfway through cooking. Turn off the oven, allow to cool for about 1 hour, then remove and cool completely before discarding the lining paper.

6 Beat the butter, confectioners' sugar, and cocoa until smooth and creamy, adding the milk or cream to form a soft consistency.

7 Set aside about a quarter of the berries to decorate. Spread one meringue with a third of the cream, and top with a third of the remaining berries. Repeat with the other meringue circles, cream, and berries.

8 Sprinkle with the toasted slivered almonds and the remaining berries. Sprinkle with confectioners' sugar, and serve.

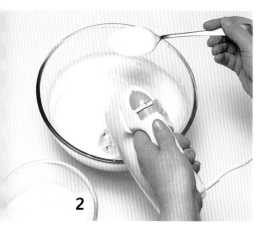

2

6

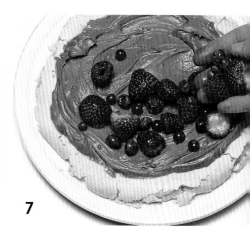

7

Orange Fruit Cake

INGREDIENTS

Cuts into 10–12 slices

Orange Cake:
2 cups self-rising flour
2 tsp. baking powder
1 cup superfine sugar
1 cup (2 sticks) butter, softened
4 extra-large eggs
grated zest of 1 orange
2 tbsp. orange juice
2–3 tbsp. Cointreau
1 cup chopped nuts
cherries, blueberries, raspberries, and
   mint sprigs to decorate
confectioners' sugar, to
   dust (optional)

For the filling:
2 cups heavy cream
⅓ cup Greek yogurt
½ tsp. vanilla extract
2–3 tbsp. Cointreau
1 tbsp. confectioners' sugar
3½ cups orange fruits, such as
   mango, peach, nectarine, papaya,
   and yellow plums

1. Preheat the oven to 350°F. Lightly grease and line the base of a 10-inch tube pan or springform pan with nonstick parchment paper.

2. Sift the flour and baking powder into a large bowl, then stir in the sugar. Make a well in the center and add the butter, eggs, grated zest, and orange juice. Beat until blended and a smooth batter is formed. Turn into the pan and smooth the top.

3. Bake in the preheated oven for 35–45 minutes or until golden and the sides begin to shrink from the edge of the pan. Remove, cool before removing from the pan, and discard the lining paper.

4. Using a serrated knife, cut the cake horizontally about one-third from the top and remove the top layer of the cake. If not using a tube pan, scoop out a center ring of sponge cake from the top third and the bottom two-thirds of the layer, making a hollow tunnel. Set aside for a trifle or other dessert. Sprinkle the cut sides with the Cointreau.

5. For the filling, whip the cream and yogurt with the vanilla extract, Cointreau, and confectioners' sugar until soft peaks form.

6. Chop the orange fruits and fold into the cream. Spoon some of this mixture onto the bottom cake layer, mounding it slightly. Transfer to a serving plate.

7. Cover with the top layer of sponge cake and spread the remaining cream mixture over the top of the cake. Press the nuts into the sides of the cake and decorate the top with the cherries, blueberries, and raspberries. If desired, dust top with confectioners' sugar, and serve.

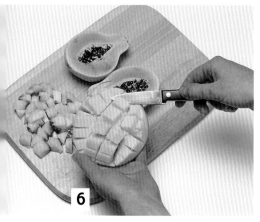

6

7

7

Chocolate Mousse Cake

INGREDIENTS

Cuts into 8–10 slices

For the cake:
1 lb. semisweet dark
  chocolate, chopped
½ cup (1 stick) butter, softened
3 tbsp. brandy
9 extra-large eggs, separated
½ cup plus 2 tbsp.
  superfine sugar

Chocolate glaze:
1 cup heavy cream
8 oz. semisweet dark
  chocolate, chopped
2 tbsp. brandy
1 tbsp. light cream and white
  chocolate curls, to decorate

FOOD FACT
Wonderfully delicious served with a fruit compote—try making cherry compote using either fresh cherries, if in season, or otherwise canned in fruit juice. Pit the cherries, drain, and then simmer on a low heat with a little apple juice until reduced.

1 Preheat the oven to 350°F. Lightly grease and line the bases of two 8-inch round springform pans with parchment paper. Melt the chocolate and butter in a bowl set over a saucepan of simmering water. Stir until smooth. Remove from the heat, and stir in the brandy.

2 Beat the egg yolks and the sugar, setting aside 2 tablespoons of the sugar, until thick and creamy. Slowly beat in the chocolate mixture until smooth and well blended. Beat the egg whites until soft peaks form, then sprinkle over the remaining sugar, and continue beating until stiff but not dry.

3 Fold a large spoonful of the egg whites into the chocolate mixture. Gently fold in the remaining egg whites. Divide about two thirds of the mixture evenly between the pans, tapping to distribute the mixture evenly. Set aside the remaining third of the chocolate mousse mixture for the filling. Bake in the preheated oven for about 20 minutes or until well risen and set. Remove and cool for at least 1 hour.

4 Loosen the edges of the cake layers with a knife. Using your fingertips, lightly press the crusty edges down. Pour the rest of the mousse over one layer, spreading until even. Carefully unclip the side, remove the other cake from the pan, and gently invert onto the mousse, bottom-side up to make a flat top layer. Discard the lining paper and chill for 4–6 hours or until set.

5 To make the glaze, melt the cream and chocolate with the brandy in a heavy-based saucepan and stir until smooth. Cool until thickened. Unclip the side of the mousse cake and place on a wire rack. Pour over half the glaze and spread to cover. Allow to set, then decorate with chocolate curls. To serve, heat the remaining glaze, pour it around each slice, and dot with cream.

1

2

4

Desserts

These recipes extend from the simple to the sophisticated and can thus provide the perfect conclusion to a range of occasions. From family favorites such as Jam Roly Poly and Crunchy Rhubarb Crisp to luxurious choices such as Chocolate Raspberry Pastry, there is something to satisfy everyone.

Iced Chocolate & Raspberry Mousse

INGREDIENTS

Serves 4

12 sponge ladyfingers

$\frac{1}{3}$ cup orange juice

2 tbsp. Grand Marnier or orange-
 flavored liqueur

1 cup heavy cream

6 oz. semisweet dark chocolate,
 broken into small pieces

2 cups frozen raspberries

6 tbsp. confectioners' sugar, sifted

unsweetened cocoa, for dusting

To decorate:
fresh whole raspberries

mint leaves

grated white chocolate

1 Break the ladyfingers into small pieces and divide among four individual glass dishes. Blend together the orange juice and Grand Marnier, then drizzle evenly over the ladyfingers. Cover with plastic wrap and chill in the refrigerator for about 30 minutes.

2 Meanwhile, place the cream in a small, heavy saucepan and heat gently, stirring occasionally until boiling. Remove the saucepan from the heat, then add the pieces of semisweet dark chocolate and allow to stand untouched for about 7 minutes. Using a whisk, beat the chocolate and cream together until the chocolate has melted and is well blended and completely smooth. Let cool slightly.

3 Place the frozen raspberries and confectioners' sugar into a food processor or blender, and blend until coarsely crushed.

4 Fold the crushed raspberries into the cream and chocolate mixture and mix lightly until well blended. Spoon over the chilled ladyfingers. Lightly dust with a little unsweetened cocoa and decorate with whole raspberries, mint leaves, and grated white chocolate. Serve immediately.

HELPFUL HINT
Remove the raspberries from the freezer about 20 minutes before you need to puree them. This will soften them slightly, but they will still be frozen.

1

2

3

Chocolate Fudge Sundae

INGREDIENTS

Serves 2

For the chocolate fudge sauce:

3 oz. semisweet dark chocolate,
  broken into pieces
2 cups heavy cream
³/₄ cup superfine sugar
¹/₄ cup all-purpose flour
pinch salt
1 tbsp. unsalted butter
1 tsp. vanilla extract

For the sundae:

1 cup raspberries, fresh or thawed
  if frozen
3 scoops vanilla ice cream
3 scoops homemade chocolate
  ice cream (*see* page 118)
2 tbsp. toasted, slivered almonds
wafers, to serve

1 To make the chocolate fudge sauce, place the chocolate and cream in a heavy saucepan and heat gently until the chocolate has melted into the cream. Stir until smooth. Mix the sugar with the flour and salt, then stir in sufficient chocolate mixture to make a smooth paste.

2 Gradually blend the remaining melted chocolate mixture into the paste, then pour into a clean saucepan. Cook over a low heat, stirring frequently until smooth and thick. Remove from the heat and add the butter and vanilla extract. Stir until smooth, then cool slightly.

3 To make the sundae, crush the raspberries lightly with a fork and set aside. Spoon a little of the chocolate sauce into the bottom of two sundae glasses. Add a layer of crushed raspberries, then a scoop each of vanilla and chocolate ice cream.

4 Top each one with a scoop of the vanilla ice cream. Pour over the sauce, sprinkle over the almonds, and serve with a wafer.

HELPFUL HINT

Ice cream will keep for up to 2 months in the freezer if kept below 0°F. If using homemade ice cream, allow to soften in the refrigerator for at least 30 minutes before using.

2

3

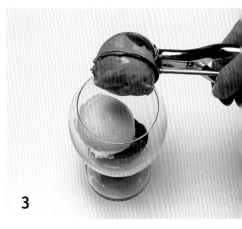
3

Chocolate Ice Cream

INGREDIENTS

Makes 4 cups

2 cups light cream
7 oz. semisweet dark chocolate
2 large eggs
2 large egg yolks
½ cup superfine sugar
1 tsp. vanilla extract
1 cup heavy cream

To serve:

chopped nuts
coarsely grated white and semisweet
  dark chocolate
a few cherries

HELPFUL HINT

When beating the ice cream, expect it to melt a little. This is what should happen. Beating is necessary to break down any large ice crystals that have formed so that the finished ice cream is smooth rather than grainy or icy.

1 Place the light cream and chocolate in a heavy saucepan, and heat gently until the chocolate has melted. Stir until smooth. Take care not to let the mixture boil. Remove from the heat.

2 Beat the eggs, egg yolks, and all but 1 tablespoon of the sugar together in a bowl until thick and pale.

3 Beat the warmed light cream and chocolate mixture with the vanilla extract into the custard mixture. Place the bowl over a saucepan of simmering water and continue beating until the mixture thickens and coats the back of a spoon. To test, lift the spoon out of the mixture and draw a clean finger through the mixture coating the spoon; if it leaves a clean line, then it is ready.

4 Stand the bowl in cold water to cool. Sprinkle the surface with the sugar to prevent a skin from forming while it is cooling. Whip the heavy cream until soft peaks form, then beat into the cooled chocolate custard.

5 Turn the ice-cream mixture into a rigid plastic container and freeze for 1 hour. Beat the ice cream thoroughly with a wooden spoon to break up all the ice crystals, then return to the freezer.

6 Continue to freeze for an additional hour, then remove and beat again. Repeat this process once or twice more, then leave the ice cream in the freezer until firm. Allow to soften in the refrigerator for at least 30 minutes before serving.

7 Remove from the refrigerator, then sprinkle over the chopped nuts and grated chocolate, and serve with cherries.

3

4

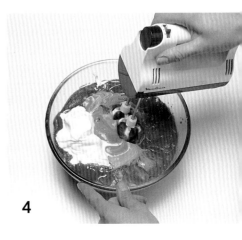

4

White Chocolate Terrine with Red Fruit Compote

INGREDIENTS

Cuts into 8 slices

8 oz. white chocolate

1 cup heavy cream

1 cup cream cheese

2 tbsp. finely grated orange zest

$\frac{1}{2}$ cup superfine sugar

3 cups mixed summer fruits, such as
  strawberries, blueberries,
  and raspberries

1 tbsp. Cointreau or
  orange-flavored liqueur

sprigs of fresh mint, to decorate

1 Lightly grease and line a loaf pan with plastic wrap, taking care to keep the plastic wrap as wrinkle-free as possible. Break the white chocolate into small pieces, and place in a heatproof bowl set over a saucepan of gently simmering water. Leave for 20 minutes or until melted, then remove from the heat and stir until smooth. Let cool.

2 Whip the cream until soft peaks form. Beat the cream cheese until soft and creamy, then beat in the grated orange zest and $\frac{1}{4}$ cup of the sugar. Mix well, then fold in the whipped cream and then the cooled melted white chocolate.

3 Spoon the mixture into the prepared loaf pan and level the surface. Place in the freezer and freeze for at least 4 hours or until frozen. Once frozen, remember to return the freezer to its normal setting.

4 Place the fruit, along with the remaining sugar, in a heavy saucepan and heat gently, stirring occasionally until the sugar has dissolved and the juices from the fruit are just beginning to run. Add the Cointreau.

5 Dip the loaf pan into hot water for 30 seconds and invert onto a serving plate. Carefully remove the pan and plastic wrap. Decorate with sprigs of mint and serve sliced with the fruit compote.

HELPFUL HINT

Pour some boiled water into a tall jug and dip your knife into it for a few seconds. Dry the knife and use to slice the terrine, repeating the dipping when necessary.

2

3

4

Chocolate Fruit Tiramisu

INGREDIENTS

Serves 4

2 ripe passion fruit
2 fresh nectarines or peaches
³/₄ cup sponge ladyfingers
1 cup amaretto cookies
5 tbsp. amaretto liqueur
6 tbsp. prepared black coffee
1 cup mascarpone cheese
2 cups ready-made custard
7 oz. semisweet dark chocolate,
   finely chopped or grated
2 tbsp. unsweetened cocoa, sifted

FOOD FACT

Mascarpone cheese is an Italian cream cheese with a very thick, creamy texture. It is a classic ingredient of tiramisu. Here, it is mixed with a custard sauce, which gives it a lighter texture.

1 Cut the passion fruit, scoop out the seeds, and set aside. Plunge the nectarines or peaches into boiling water and leave for 2–3 minutes. Carefully remove the nectarines from the water, cut in half, and remove the pits. Peel off the skin, chop the flesh finely, and set aside.

2 Break the sponge ladyfingers and amaretto cookies in half. Place the amaretto liqueur and prepared black coffee into a shallow dish and stir well. Place half the sponge ladyfingers and amaretto cookies into the amaretto and coffee mixture, and soak for 30 seconds.

3 Lift out both cookies from the liquor and arrange in the bottom of four deep individual glass dishes. Cream the mascarpone cheese until soft and creamy, then slowly beat in the custard and mix well together. Spoon half the mascarpone mixture over the cookies in the dishes and sprinkle with 4 oz. of the finely chopped or grated semisweet dark chocolate.

4 Arrange half the passion fruit seeds and the chopped nectarine or peaches over the chocolate, and sprinkle with half the sifted unsweetened cocoa.

5 Place the remaining cookies in the remaining coffee-liqueur mixture and soak for 30 seconds, then arrange on top of the fruit and unsweetened cocoa. Top with the remaining chopped or grated chocolate, nectarine or peach, and the mascarpone cheese mixture, piling the mascarpone high in the dishes.

6 Chill in the refrigerator for 1½ hours, then spoon the remaining passion fruit seeds and unsweetened cocoa over the desserts. Chill in the refrigerator for 30 minutes and serve.

1

2

3

Crème Brûlée with Sugared Raspberries

INGREDIENTS

Serves 6

2¹/₂ cups fresh whipping cream
4 large egg yolks
6 tbsp. superfine sugar
¹/₂ tsp. vanilla extract
2 tbsp. turbinado sugar
1 generous cup fresh raspberries

HELPFUL HINT

Most chefs use blowtorches to brown the sugar in step 6, because this is the quickest way to caramelize the top of the dessert. Take great care if using a blowtorch, especially when lighting. Otherwise, use the broiler, making sure that it is very hot and the dessert is thoroughly chilled before caramelizing the sugar topping. This will stop the custard underneath from melting.

1 Preheat the oven to 300°F. Pour the cream into a bowl and place over a saucepan of gently simmering water. Heat gently but do not allow to boil.

2 Meanwhile, beat together the egg yolks, 4 tablespoons of the superfine sugar, and the vanilla extract. When the cream is warm, pour it over egg mixture, beating briskly until it is mixed completely.

3 Pour into six individual baking dishes and place in a roasting pan. Fill the pan with enough water to come halfway up the sides of the dishes.

4 Bake in the preheated oven for about 1 hour or until the custards are set. (To test if set, carefully insert a knife into the center; if the knife comes out clean, they are set.)

5 Remove the custards from the roasting pan and let cool. Chill in the refrigerator, preferably overnight.

6 Sprinkle the turbinado sugar over the top of each dish and place the custards under a preheated hot broiler.

7 When the sugar has caramelized and turned deep brown, remove from the heat and cool. Chill the custards in the refrigerator for 2–3 hours before serving.

8 Toss the raspberries in the remaining superfine sugar and sprinkle over the top of each dish. Serve with a little extra cream, if desired.

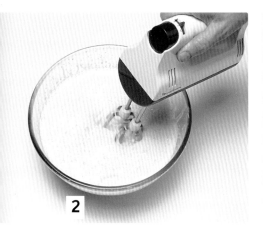

2

5

7

Chocolate Trifle

INGREDIENTS

Serves 4

1¹/₂ chocolate jelly rolls

4 tbsp. strawberry jam

3 tbsp. medium sherry

3 tbsp. brandy

3 cups fresh strawberries

2 small mangoes, peeled, pitted, and diced

7 oz. semisweet dark chocolate

2 tbsp. custard powder

2 tbsp. granulated sugar

1¹/₄ cups whole milk

1 cup mascarpone cheese

1 cup heavy cream

3 tbsp. toasted slivered almonds

1 Slice the chocolate jelly roll thickly, and spread each slice with a little strawberry jam. Place the jelly-roll slices in the bottom of a trifle dish or glass bowl. Sprinkle over the sherry and brandy and let stand for 10 minutes to let the sherry and brandy soak into the jelly roll. Slice half the strawberries and sprinkle evenly over the jelly roll with half the diced mangoes.

2 Break the chocolate into small pieces and place in a small heatproof bowl set over a saucepan of gently simmering water. Heat gently, stirring occasionally, until the chocolate has melted and is smooth and free from lumps.

3 Blend the custard powder, sugar, and milk to a smooth paste in a bowl, then pour into a heavy saucepan. Place over a gentle heat and cook, stirring constantly, until the custard is smooth and thick. Add the melted chocolate and stir until smooth and blended. Remove from the heat and let cool. Stir in the mascarpone cheese.

4 Spoon the custard mixture over the fruit and chill in the refrigerator for 1 hour. Whip the cream until soft peaks form and pile over the top of the set custard. Sprinkle over the toasted slivered almonds and decorate with the remaining whole strawberries and diced mangoes.

TASTY TIP

If you prefer, use fresh custard sauce. Heat gently, then stir in the chocolate and mascarpone cheese. Omit the custard powder, sugar, and milk.

1

3

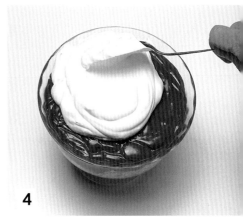

4

Chocolate Cream Puffs

INGREDIENTS

Serves 4

For the pastry:

²/₃ cup water
4 tbsp. butter
²/₃ cup all-purpose flour, sifted
2 large eggs, lightly beaten

For the custard sauce:

1¹/₄ cups milk
pinch freshly grated nutmeg
3 large egg yolks
¹/₄ cup superfine sugar
2 tbsp. all-purpose flour, sifted
2 tbsp. cornstarch, sifted

For the sauce:

³/₄ cup firmly packed brown sugar
²/₃ cup boiling water
1 tsp. instant coffee
1 tbsp. unsweetened cocoa
1 tbsp. brandy
6 tbsp. butter
1 tbsp. light corn syrup

1 Preheat the oven to 425°F. Lightly grease two cookie sheets. For the pastry, place the water and the butter in a heavy saucepan and bring to a boil. Remove from the heat and beat in the flour. Return to the heat and cook for 1 minute or until the mixture forms a ball in the center of the saucepan.

2 Remove from the heat and let cool slightly, then gradually beat in the eggs, a little at a time, beating well after each addition. Once all the eggs have been added, beat until the paste is smooth and glossy. Pipe or spoon 20 small balls onto the cookie sheets, allowing plenty of room for expansion.

3 Bake in the preheated oven for 25 minutes or until well risen and golden brown. Reduce the oven temperature to 350°F. Make a hole in each ball and continue to bake for an additional 5 minutes. Remove from the oven and let cool.

4 For the custard sauce, place the milk and nutmeg in a small heavy saucepan, and bring to a boil. In another small heavy saucepan, beat together the egg yolks, sugar, and the flours, then beat in the hot milk. Bring to a boil and simmer, beating constantly for 2 minutes. Cover and let cool.

5 Spoon the custard into the profiteroles and then arrange the profiteroles on a large serving dish. Place all the sauce ingredients in a small, heavy saucepan and bring to a boil, then simmer for 10 minutes. Remove the saucepan from the heat and let cool slightly before serving with the chocolate profiteroles.

1

2

5

White Chocolate Éclairs

INGREDIENTS

Serves 4–6

4 tbsp. unsalted butter

²⁄₃ cup all-purpose flour, sifted

2 large eggs, lightly beaten

6 ripe passion fruit

1 cup heavy cream

3 tbsp. kirsch

1 tbsp. confectioners' sugar

4 oz. white chocolate, broken
  into pieces

HELPFUL HINT

Passion fruit are increasingly available in supermarkets. They are small, round, purplish fruits that should have quite wrinkled skins. Smooth ones are not ripe and will have little juice and poor flavor.

1 Preheat the oven to 375°F. Lightly grease a baking sheet. Place the butter and ²⁄₃ cup of water in a saucepan, and heat until the butter has melted, then bring to a boil.

2 Remove the saucepan from the heat and immediately add the flour all at once, beating with a wooden spoon until the mixture forms a ball in the center of the saucepan. Let cool for 3 minutes.

3 Add the eggs a little at a time, beating well after each addition until the paste is smooth, shiny, and of a piping consistency. Spoon the mixture into a decorating bag fitted with a plain tip. Sprinkle the greased baking pan with a little water. Pipe the mixture onto the baking pan in 3-inch lengths, using a small, sharp knife to cut each pastry length neatly.

4 Bake in the preheated oven for 18–20 minutes or until well risen and golden. Make a slit along the side of each éclair to let the steam escape. Return the éclairs to the oven for an additional 2 minutes to dry out. Transfer to a wire rack and let cool.

5 Halve the passion fruit, and using a small spoon, scoop the pulp of 4 of the fruits into a bowl. Add the cream, kirsch, and confectioners' sugar, and whip until the cream holds it shape. Spoon or pipe into the éclairs.

6 Melt the chocolate in a small heatproof bowl set over a saucepan of simmering water and stir until smooth. Let the chocolate cool slightly, then spread over the top of the éclairs. Scoop the seeds and pulp out of the remaining passion fruit. Strain. Use the juice to drizzle around the éclairs when serving.

2

4

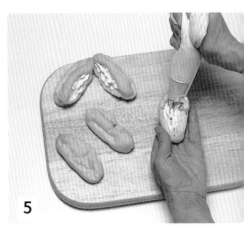

5

Chocolate & Rum Truffles

INGREDIENTS

Makes 44

For the chocolate truffles:

8 oz. semisweet dark chocolate

2 tbsp. butter, softened

2 large egg yolks

2 tsp. brandy or kirsch

2 tsp. heavy cream

24 maraschino cherries, drained

2 tbsp. unsweetened cocoa, sifted

For the rum truffles:

4 oz. semisweet dark chocolate

2 tbsp. rum

$\frac{1}{2}$ cup heavy cream

$\frac{1}{2}$ cup ground almonds

2 tbsp. confectioners' sugar, sifted

TASTY TIP

These truffles are so easy to make, they are great to give as gifts. Roll some in confectioners' sugar, as above, and roll others in cocoa. Arrange in a gift box in a checkerboard pattern.

1 For the chocolate truffles, break the chocolate into pieces and place in a heatproof bowl set over a saucepan of gently simmering water. Leave for 20 minutes or until the chocolate has melted. Stir until the chocolate is smooth, and remove from the heat. Let stand for about 6 minutes.

2 Beat the butter, egg yolks, brandy or kirsch, and heavy cream together until smooth. Stir the melted chocolate into the butter and egg yolk mixture and stir until thick. Cover and let cool for about 30 minutes. Chill in the refrigerator for 1½ hours or until firm.

3 Divide the truffle mixture into 24 pieces and mold around the drained cherries. Roll in the unsweetened cocoa until evenly coated. Place the truffles in petit-four paper cases and chill in the refrigerator for 2 hours before serving.

4 To make the rum truffles, break the chocolate into small pieces and place in a heavy saucepan with the cream and rum. Heat gently until the chocolate has melted, then stir until smooth. Stir in the ground almonds, pour into a small bowl, and chill in the refrigerator for at least 6 hours or until the mixture is thick.

5 Remove the truffles from the refrigerator and shape small spoonfuls, about the size of a cherry, into balls. Roll in the sifted confectioners' sugar and place in petit-four paper cases. Store the truffles in the refrigerator until ready to serve.

1

2

3

Chocolate Meringue Nest with Fruity Filling

INGREDIENTS

Makes 8

1 cup toasted hazelnuts
½ cup superfine sugar
3 oz. semisweet dark chocolate, broken into pieces
2 large egg whites
pinch salt
1 tsp. cornstarch
½ tsp. white wine vinegar
chocolate curls, to decorate

For the filling:

½ cup heavy cream
⅔ cup mascarpone cheese
prepared summer fruits, such as strawberries, raspberries, and red currants

HELPFUL HINT

To make chocolate curls, melt chocolate over hot water, then pour onto a cool surface. Leave until just set but not hard, then using a large cook's knife, push the blade at an angle across the surface of the chocolate to form curls.

1 Preheat the oven to 225°F, and line a baking pan with nonstick parchment paper. Place the hazelnuts and 2 tablespoons of the sugar in a food processor, and blend to a powder. Add the chocolate and blend again until the chocolate is coarsely chopped.

2 In a clean, grease-free bowl, beat the egg whites and salt until soft peaks form. Gradually beat in the remaining sugar a teaspoonful at a time, and continue to beat until the meringue is stiff and shiny. Fold in the cornstarch and the white wine vinegar with the chocolate and hazelnut mixture.

3 Spoon the mixture into eight mounds, about 4 inches in diameter, on the parchment paper. Make a hollow in each mound, then place in the preheated oven. Cook for 1½ hours, then switch the oven off and leave in the oven until cool.

4 To make the filling, whip the cream until soft peaks form. In another bowl, beat the mascarpone cheese until it is softened, then mix with the cream. Spoon the mixture into the meringue nests and top with the fresh fruits. Decorate with a few chocolate curls, and serve.

1

2

3

Chocolate Marshmallow Pie

INGREDIENTS

Cuts into 6 slices

14 Graham crackers
6 tbsp. butter, melted
6 oz. semisweet dark chocolate
20 marshmallows
1 large egg, separated
1 cup heavy cream

1 Place the crackers in a plastic container, and crush finely with a rolling pin. Alternatively, place in a food processor and blend until fine crumbs are formed.

2 Melt the butter in a medium-sized saucepan, add the crumbs and mix together. Press into the bottom of the prepared pan and let cool in the refrigerator.

3 Melt 4 oz. of the chocolate with the marshmallows and 2 tablespoons water in a saucepan over a gentle heat, stirring constantly. Let cool slightly, then stir in the egg yolk, beat well, then return to the refrigerator until cool.

4 Beat the egg white until stiff and standing in peaks, then fold into the chocolate mixture.

5 Lightly whip the cream and fold three-quarters of the cream into the chocolate mixture. Set the remainder aside. Spoon the chocolate cream into the flan shell and chill in the refrigerator until set.

6 When ready to serve, spoon the remaining cream over the chocolate pie, swirling in a decorative pattern. Grate the remaining semisweet dark chocolate and sprinkle over the cream, then serve.

TASTY TIP
Replace the Graham crackers with an equal amount of chocolate-covered cookies to make a quick change to this recipe.

2

3

5

Lattice Syrup Tart

INGREDIENTS

Cuts into 4 slices

For the pastry:
1½ cups all-purpose flour
3 tbsp. butter
3 tbsp. shortening

For the filling:
³/₄ cup light corn syrup
finely grated zest and juice of 1 lemon
1½ cups fresh white bread crumbs
1 medium egg, beaten

1 Preheat the oven to 375°F. Make the pastry by placing the flour, butter, and shortening in a food processor. Blend in short, sharp bursts until the mixture resembles fine bread crumbs. Remove from the processor, and place on a pastry board or in a large bowl.

2 Stir in enough cold water to make a dough, and knead in a large bowl or on a floured surface until smooth and pliable.

3 Roll out the pastry and use to line a 8-inch, loose-bottomed, fluted tart pan. Put aside pastry trimmings for decoration. Chill for 30 minutes.

4 Meanwhile, to make the filling, place the corn syrup in a saucepan and warm gently with the lemon zest and juice. Tip the bread crumbs into the pastry shell, and pour the syrup mixture over the top.

5 Roll the pastry trimmings out on a lightly floured surface and cut into 6–8 thin strips. Lightly dampen the pastry edge of the tart, then place the strips across the filling in a lattice pattern. Brush the ends of the strips with water, and seal to the edge of the tart. Brush a little beaten egg over the pastry and bake in the preheated oven for 25 minutes or until the filling is just set. Serve hot or cold.

TASTY TIP
Why not replace the bread crumbs with the same amount of shredded coconut?

1

4

5

Chocolate, Orange & Pine Nut Tart

INGREDIENTS

Cuts into 8–10 slices

For the sweet piecrust:

1¼ cups all-purpose flour

½ tsp. salt

3–4 tbsp. confectioners' sugar

½ cup (1 stick) unsalted butter, diced

2 large egg yolks, beaten

½ tsp. vanilla extract

For the filling:

4 oz. semisweet dark
  chocolate, chopped

⅔ cup lightly toasted pine nuts

2 extra-large eggs

1 tbsp. grated orange zest

1 tbsp. Cointreau or
  orange-flavored liqueur

1 cup heavy cream

2 tbsp. orange marmalade

1. Preheat the oven to 400°F. Place the flour, salt, and sugar in a food processor with the butter and blend briefly. Add the egg yolks, 2 tablespoons of iced water, and the vanilla extract, and blend until a soft dough is formed. Remove and knead until smooth, wrap in plastic wrap, and chill in the refrigerator for 1 hour.

2. Lightly grease a 9-inch springform flan pan. Roll the dough out on a lightly floured surface to an 11-inch round, and use to line the pan. Press into the sides of the flan pan, crimp the edges, prick the bottom with a fork, and chill in the refrigerator for 1 hour. Bake blind in the preheated oven for 10 minutes. Remove and place on a large baking pan. Reduce the oven temperature to 375°F.

3. To make the filling, sprinkle the chocolate and the pine nuts evenly over the bottom of the pie crust. Beat the eggs, orange zest, Cointreau, and cream in a bowl until well blended, then pour over the chocolate and pine nuts.

4. Bake in the oven for 30 minutes or until the pastry is golden and the custard mixture is just set. Transfer to a wire rack to cool slightly. Heat the marmalade with 1 tablespoon of water and brush over the tart. Serve warm or at room temperature.

FOOD FACT

Cointreau is an orange-flavored liqueur and is used in many recipes. You could substitute Grand Marnier or any other orange liqueur, if you prefer.

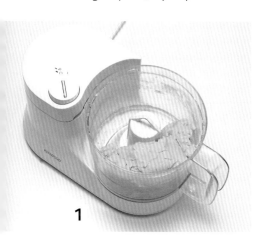

1

2

3

Chocolate Pecan Pie

INGREDIENTS

Cuts into 8–10 slices

8 oz. prepared sweet piecrust dough
(*see* page 140)

1³/₄ cups pecan halves

4 oz. semisweet dark
chocolate, chopped

2 tbsp. butter, diced

3 large eggs

¹/₂ cup firmly packed brown sugar

¹/₂ cup corn syrup

2 tsp. vanilla extract

vanilla ice cream, to serve

1 Preheat the oven to 350°F. Roll the prepared dough out on a lightly floured surface and use to line a 10-inch pie plate. Roll the trimmings out and use to make a decorative edge around the pie, then chill in the refrigerator for 1 hour.

2 Set aside about 60 perfect pecan halves or enough to cover the top of the pie, then coarsely chop the remainder and set aside. Melt the chocolate and butter in a small saucepan over a low heat or in the microwave, and set aside.

3 Beat the eggs and brush the bottom and sides of the pie shell with a little of the beaten egg. Beat the sugar, corn syrup, and vanilla extract into the beaten eggs. Add the pecans, then beat in the chocolate mixture.

4 Pour the filling into the pie shell and arrange the pecan halves in concentric circles over the top. Bake in the preheated oven for 45–55 minutes or until the filling is well risen and just set. If the pastry edge begins to brown too quickly, cover with strips of foil. Remove from the oven and serve with ice cream.

HELPFUL HINT

The pie shell in this recipe is not baked blind, but the pie does not become soggy because of the long cooking time, which allows the pastry to become crisp.

1

3

4

Pear & Chocolate Custard Tart

INGREDIENTS

Cuts into 6–8 slices

For the chocolate piecrust:

½ cup (1 stick) unsalted
  butter, softened

⅓ cup superfine sugar

2 tsp. vanilla extract

1½ cups all-purpose flour, sifted

⅓ cup unsweetened cocoa

whipped cream, to serve

For the filling:

4 oz. semisweet dark
  chocolate, chopped

1 cup heavy cream

¼ cup superfine sugar

1 extra-large egg

1 extra-large egg yolk

1 tbsp. crème de cacao

3 ripe pears

HELPFUL HINT

Chocolate dough is very soft, so rolling it between sheets of plastic wrap will make it much easier to handle without having to add a lot of extra flour.

1. Preheat the oven to 375°F. To make the piecrust, put the butter, sugar, and vanilla extract into a food processor, and blend until creamy. Add the flour and unsweetened cocoa, and process until a soft dough forms. Remove the dough, wrap in plastic wrap, and chill in the refrigerator for at least 1 hour.

2. Roll out the dough between two sheets of plastic wrap to an 11-inch round. Peel off top sheet of plastic wrap and invert the dough round into a lightly greased 9-inch springform cake pan, easing the dough into bottom and sides. Prick bottom with a fork, then chill for 1 hour.

3. Place a sheet of nonstick parchment paper and baking beans in the shell, and bake blind in the preheated oven for 10 minutes. Remove the parchment paper and beans, and bake for an additional 5 minutes. Remove and cool.

4. To make the filling, heat the chocolate, cream, and half the sugar in a medium saucepan over a low heat, stirring until melted and smooth. Remove from the heat and cool slightly before beating in the egg, egg yolk, and crème de cacao. Spread evenly over the bottom piecrust.

5. Peel the pears, then cut each pear in half and carefully remove the core. Cut each half crosswise into thin slices, and arrange over the custard sauce, gently fanning the slices toward the center and pressing into the chocolate custard sauce. Bake in the oven for 10 minutes.

6. Reduce the oven temperature to 350°F, and sprinkle the surface evenly with the remaining sugar. Bake in the oven for 20–25 minutes or until the custard is set and the pears are tender and glazed. Remove from the oven and let cool slightly. Cut into slices, then serve with spoonfuls of whipped cream.

1

2

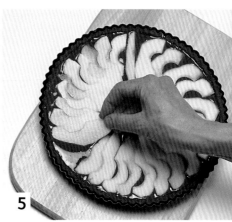

5

Double Chocolate Banana Pie

INGREDIENTS

Cuts into 8 slices

2 14-oz. cans sweetened
  condensed milk
6 oz. semisweet dark
  chocolate, chopped
2 cups heavy cream
1 tbsp. light corn syrup
2 tbsp. butter, diced
5 oz. white chocolate, grated or
  finely chopped
1 tsp. vanilla extract
2–3 ripe bananas
unsweetened cocoa, for dusting

For the ginger crumb crust:

24–26 ginger cookies,
  coarsely crushed
7 tbsp. butter, melted
1–2 tbsp. sugar, or to taste
½ tsp. ground ginger

TASTY TIP

Do not assemble the pie more than 2–3 hours before serving, as it will go too soft.

1 Preheat the oven to 375°F. Place the condensed milk in a heavy saucepan and place over a gentle heat. Bring to a boil, stirring constantly. Boil gently for about 3–5 minutes or until golden. Remove from the heat and let cool.

2 To make the ginger crumb crust, place the cookies with the melted butter, sugar, and ginger in a food processor, and blend together. Press into the sides and bottom of a 9-inch springform cake pan. Chill in the refrigerator for 15–20 minutes, then bake in the preheated oven for 5–6 minutes. Remove from the oven and let cool.

3 Melt the dark chocolate in a medium-sized saucepan with ½ cup of the heavy cream, the corn syrup, and the butter over a low heat. Stir until smooth. Carefully pour into the crumb crust, tilting the pan to distribute the chocolate layer evenly. Chill in the refrigerator for at least 1 hour or until set.

4 Heat ½ cup of the remaining cream until hot, then add all the white chocolate and stir until melted and smooth. Stir in the vanilla extract and strain into a bowl. Let cool to room temperature.

5 Scrape the cooked condensed milk into a bowl and beat until smooth, adding a little of the remaining cream if too thick. Spread over the chocolate layer, then slice the bananas and arrange them evenly over the top.

6 Beat the remaining cream until soft peaks form. Stir a spoonful of the cream into the white chocolate mixture, then fold in the remaining cream. Spread over the bananas, swirling to the edge. Dust with a little unsweetened cocoa and chill the pie in the refrigerator until ready to serve.

3

5

6

Chocolate Apricot Linzer Torte

INGREDIENTS

Cuts into 10–12 slices

For the chocolate almond piecrust:

³/₄ cup whole blanched almonds

¹/₂ cup caster sugar

1³/₄ cups all-purpose flour

2 tbsp. unsweetened cocoa

1 tsp. ground cinnamon

¹/₂ tsp. salt

1 tbsp. orange zest

1 cup (2 sticks) unsalted butter, diced

2–3 tbsp. ice water

For the filling:

1 cup apricot jam

3 oz. milk chocolate, chopped

confectioners' sugar, for dusting

1 Preheat the oven to 190°F. Lightly grease an 11-inch cake pan. Place the almonds and half the sugar into a food processor and blend until finely ground. Add the remaining sugar, flour, unsweetened cocoa, cinnamon, salt, and orange zest, and blend again. Add the diced butter and blend in short bursts to form coarse crumbs. Add the water, 1 tablespoon at a time, until the mixture starts to come together.

2 Turn onto a lightly floured surface, knead lightly, and roll out. Then using your fingertips, press half the dough onto the bottom and sides of the pan. Prick the bottom with a fork and chill in the refrigerator. Roll out the remaining dough between two pieces of plastic wrap to a 12-inch round. Slide the round onto a cookie sheet and chill in the refrigerator for 30 minutes.

3 For the filling, spread the apricot jam evenly over the chilled pie bottom and sprinkle with the chopped chocolate.

4 Slide the dough round onto a lightly floured surface and peel off the top layer of plastic wrap. Using a straight edge, cut the round into ¹/₂-inch strips; allow to soften until slightly flexible. Place half the strips about ¹/₂ inch apart to create a lattice pattern. Press down on each side of each crossing to accentuate the effect. Press the ends of the strips to the edge, cutting off any excess. Bake in the preheated oven for 35 minutes or until cooked. Let cool, then dust with confectioners' sugar. Serve cut into slices.

TASTY TIP

When making the dough do not allow it to form into a ball or it will become tough.

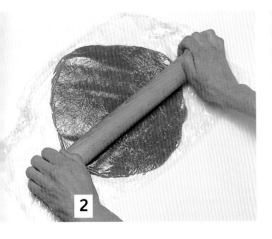

2

3

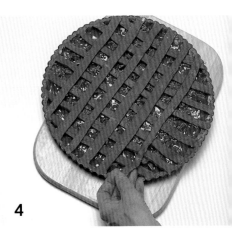

4

Chocolate Peanut Butter Pie

INGREDIENTS

Cuts into 8 slices

22–24 chocolate wafers or peanut
 butter cookies

7 tbsp. butter, melted

1–2 tbsp. sugar

1 tsp. vanilla extract

1½ tbsp. powdered gelatin

½ cup superfine sugar

1 tbsp. cornstarch

½ tsp. salt

1 cup milk

2 extra-large eggs, separated

2 extra-large egg yolks

3½ oz. semisweet dark
 chocolate, chopped

2 tbsp. rum or 2 tsp. vanilla extract

½ cup smooth peanut butter

1 cup heavy cream

chocolate curls, to decorate

1 Place the wafers or cookies, along with the melted butter, sugar, and vanilla extract, in a food processor and blend together. Press into the bottom of a 9-inch pie plate or cake pan. Chill in the refrigerator for 15–20 minutes.

2 Place 3 tablespoons of cold water in a bowl and sprinkle in the powdered gelatin. Leave until softened.

3 Blend half the superfine sugar with the cornstarch and salt in a heavy saucepan and gradually beat in the milk. Bring to a boil, then reduce the heat and boil gently for 1–2 minutes or until thickened and smooth, stirring constantly.

4 Beat all the egg yolks together, then beat in half of the hot milk mixture until blended. Beat in the remaining milk mixture, return to a clean saucepan, and cook gently until the mixture comes to a boil and thickens. Boil, stirring vigorously for 1 minute, then pour a quarter of the custard into a bowl. Add the chopped chocolate and rum or vanilla extract, and stir until the chocolate has melted and the mixture is smooth. Pour into the chocolate crust and chill in the refrigerator until set.

5 Beat the softened gelatin into the remaining custard and beat until thoroughly dissolved. Beat in the peanut butter until melted and smooth. Beat the egg whites until stiff, then beat in the remaining sugar, 1 tablespoon at a time.

6 Whip the cream until soft peaks form. Fold ½ cup of the cream into the custard, then fold in the egg whites. Spread the peanut butter cream mixture over the chocolate layer. Spread or pipe over the surface with the remaining cream, forming decorative swirls. Decorate with chocolate curls and chill in the refrigerator until ready to serve.

1

3

4

Mini Pistachio & Chocolate Strudels

INGREDIENTS

Makes 24

5 large sheets phyllo pastry

4 tbsp. butter, melted

1–2 tbsp. superfine sugar,
  for sprinkling

2 oz. melted white chocolate,
  to decorate

For the filling:

1 cup finely chopped
  unsalted pistachios

3 tbsp. superfine sugar

2 oz. semisweet dark chocolate,
  finely chopped

1–2 tsp. rose water

1 tbsp. confectioners' sugar,
  for dusting

1 Preheat the oven to 325°F. Lightly grease two large baking pans. For the filling, mix the finely chopped pistachio nuts, sugar, and dark chocolate in a bowl. Sprinkle with the rose water, stir lightly together, and set aside.

2 Cut each phyllo pastry sheet into four to make 7 x 9-inch rectangles. Place one rectangle on the work surface and brush with a little melted butter. Place another rectangle on top and brush with a little more butter. Sprinkle with a little sugar and spread about 1 spoonful of the filling along one short end. Fold the short end over the filling, then fold in the long edges and roll up. Place on the baking pan seam-side down. Continue with the remaining pastry sheets and filling until both are used.

3 Brush each strudel with the remaining melted butter, and sprinkle with a little sugar. Bake in the preheated oven for 20 minutes or until golden brown and the pastry is crisp.

4 Remove from the oven and leave on the baking pan for 2 minutes, then transfer to a wire rack. Dust with confectioners' sugar. Place the melted white chocolate in a small decorating bag fitted with a plain writing pipe and pipe squiggles over the strudel. Let set before serving.

TASTY TIP

Keep unused phyllo pastry covered with a clean, damp dishtowel to prevent it from drying out.

1

2

3

Raspberry Chocolate Ganache & Berry Tartlets

INGREDIENTS

Makes 8

1 quantity chocolate piecrust dough
  (*see* page 144)
2 cups heavy cream
$^3/_4$ cup seedless raspberry jelly
8 oz. semisweet dark
  chocolate, chopped
$6^1/_2$ cups raspberries or other
  summer berries
$^1/_4$ cup framboise liqueur
1 tbsp. superfine sugar
sour cream, to serve

1 Preheat the oven to 400°F. Make the chocolate piecrust and use to line eight 3-inch tartlet pans. Bake blind in preheated oven for 12 minutes.

2 Place $^3/_4$ cup cream and half of the raspberry jelly in a saucepan and bring to a boil, beating constantly to dissolve the jelly. Remove from the heat and add the chocolate all at once, stirring until the chocolate has melted.

3 Pour into the pastry-lined tartlet pans, shaking gently to distribute the ganache evenly. Chill in the refrigerator for 1 hour or until set.

4 Place the berries in a large, shallow bowl. Heat the remaining raspberry jelly with half the framboise liqueur over a medium heat until melted and bubbling. Drizzle over the berries and toss gently to coat.

5 Divide the berries among the tartlets, piling them up if necessary. Chill in the refrigerator until ready to serve.

6 Remove the tartlets from the refrigerator for at least 30 minutes before serving. Using an electric whisk, beat the remaining cream with the sugar and the remaining framboise liqueur until it is thick and softly peaking. Serve with the tartlets and sour cream.

TASTY TIP

Substitute an equal quantity of white chocolate for the dark chocolate, as raspberries go well with it.

1

2

3

Chocolaty Puffs

INGREDIENTS

Makes 12 large puffs

For the choux pastry:
1¼ cups all-purpose flour

2 tbsp. unsweetened cocoa

½ tsp. salt

1 tbsp. sugar

½ cup (1 stick) butter, cut into pieces

5 extra-large eggs

For the chocolate ice cream filling:
8 oz. semisweet dark
  chocolate, chopped

2 cups heavy cream

1 tbsp. superfine sugar (optional)

2 tbsp. crème de cacao (optional)

For the chocolate sauce:
8 oz. semisweet dark chocolate

1 cup heavy cream

4 tbsp. butter, diced

1–2 tbsp. light corn syrup

1 tsp. vanilla extract

1 Preheat the oven to 425°F. Lightly grease a large baking pan. To make the choux pastry, sift the flour and unsweetened cocoa together. Place 1 cup of water, the salt, sugar, and butter in a saucepan, and bring to a boil. Remove from the heat and add the flour mixture all at once, beating vigorously with a wooden spoon until the mixture forms a ball in the center of the saucepan. Return to the heat and cook for 1 minute, stirring, then allow to cool slightly.

2 Using an electric mixer, beat in 4 of the eggs, one at a time, beating well after each addition. Beat the last egg and add a little at a time until the dough is thick and shiny, and just falls from a spoon when tapped on the side of the saucepan.

3 Pipe or spoon 12 large puffs onto the prepared baking pan, leaving space between them. Cook in the preheated oven for 30–35 minutes or until puffy and golden. Remove from the oven, slice off the top third of each bun, and return to the oven for 5 minutes to dry out. Remove and let cool.

4 For the filling, heat the chocolate with ½ cup heavy cream and 1 tablespoon sugar, if desired, stirring until smooth. Let cool. Whip the remaining cream until soft peaks form, and stir in the crème de cacao, if desired. Quickly fold the cream into the chocolate, then spoon or pipe into the choux buns and place the lids on top.

5 Place all the ingredients for the chocolate sauce in a small, heavy saucepan and heat gently, stirring until the sauce is smooth. Remove from the heat and let cool, stirring occasionally until thickened. Pour over the puffs and serve immediately.

1

3

5

Rice Pudding & Chocolate Tart

INGREDIENTS

Cuts into 8 slices

1 quantity chocolate piecrust dough
 (*see* page 144)
1 tsp. unsweetened cocoa, for dusting

For the chocolate ganache:

1 cup heavy cream
1 tbsp. light corn syrup
6 oz. semisweet dark
  chocolate, chopped
1 tbsp. butter
1 tsp. vanilla extract

For the rice pudding:

4 cups milk
$\frac{1}{2}$ tsp. salt
1 vanilla pod
$\frac{1}{2}$ cup long-grain rice
1 tbsp. cornstarch
2 tbsp. sugar

To decorate:

fresh blueberries
sprigs of fresh mint

1 Preheat the oven to 400°F. Roll the chocolate dough out and use to line a 9-inch cake pan. Place a sheet of parchment paper and baking beans in the pan, and bake blind in the preheated oven for 15 minutes.

2 For the ganache, place the cream and corn syrup in a heavy saucepan, and bring to a boil. Remove from the heat and add the chocolate all at once, stirring until smooth. Beat in the butter and vanilla extract, pour into the baked pie shell, and set aside.

3 For the rice pudding, bring the milk and salt to a boil in a medium-sized saucepan. Split the vanilla pod and scrape the seeds into the milk. Add the vanilla pod, sprinkle in the rice, then bring to a boil. Reduce the heat and simmer until the rice is tender and the milk is creamy. Remove from the heat.

4 Blend the cornstarch and sugar together, then stir in 2 tablespoons of water to make a paste. Stir a little of the hot rice mixture into the cornstarch mixture, then stir the cornstarch mixture into the rice. Bring to a boil and cook, stirring constantly until thickened. Set the bottom of the saucepan into a bowl of iced water and stir until cooled and thickened. Spoon the rice pudding into the tart, smoothing the surface. Allow to set. Dust with unsweetened cocoa, decorate with a few blueberries and fresh mint sprigs, and serve.

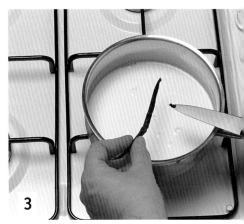

Chocolate Lemon Tartlets

INGREDIENTS

Makes 10

1 quantity chocolate piecrust dough
  (*see* page 144)
³/₄ cup heavy cream
6 oz. chopped semisweet
  dark chocolate
2 tbsp. butter, diced
1 tsp. vanilla extract
1 cup lemon curd
1 cup prepared custard sauce
1 cup light cream
¹/₂–1 tsp. almond extract

To decorate:

grated chocolate
toasted slivered almonds

TASTY TIP

Lemon curd is very easy to make. In a medium-sized heatproof bowl, mix together ³/₄ cup sugar, 2 tablespoons lemon zest, 6 tablespoons lemon juice, and 4 extra-large eggs. Add 1 stick cubed unsalted butter and place the bowl over a saucepan of gently simmering water. Stir often until thickened, about 20 minutes. Let cool and use as above.

1 Preheat the oven to 400°F. Roll the prepared dough out on a lightly floured surface and use to line 10 3-inch tartlet pans. Place a small piece of crumpled foil in each and bake blind in the preheated oven for 12 minutes. Remove from the oven and let cool.

2 Bring the cream to a boil, then remove from the heat and add the chocolate all at once. Stir until smooth and melted. Beat in the butter and vanilla extract, pour into the tartlets, and let cool.

3 Beat the lemon curd until soft, and spoon a thick layer over the chocolate in each tartlet, spreading gently to the edges. Do not chill in the refrigerator or the chocolate will be too firm.

4 Place the prepared custard sauce into a large bowl, and gradually beat in the cream and almond extract until the custard is smooth and runny.

5 To serve, spoon a little custard sauce onto a plate and place a tartlet in the center. Sprinkle with grated chocolate and almonds, then serve.

1

2

3

Fudgy Mocha Pie with Espresso Custard Sauce

INGREDIENTS

Cuts into 10 slices

4 oz. chopped semisweet
dark chocolate
½ cup (1 stick) diced butter
1 tbsp. instant espresso powder
4 extra-large eggs
1 tbsp. light corn syrup
½ cup sugar
1 tsp. ground cinnamon
3 tbsp. milk
confectioners' sugar for dusting
fresh strawberries, to serve

For the espresso custard sauce:

2–3 tbsp. instant espresso powder,
or to taste
1 cup prepared custard sauce
1 cup light cream
2 tbsp. coffee-flavored
liqueur (optional)

1. Preheat the oven to 350°F. Line with foil or lightly grease a deep 9-inch pie plate. Melt the chocolate and butter in a small saucepan over a low heat and stir until smooth, then set aside. Dissolve the instant espresso powder in 1–2 tablespoons of hot water, and set aside.

2. Beat the eggs with the corn syrup, sugar, dissolved espresso powder, cinnamon, and milk until blended. Add the melted chocolate mixture and beat until blended. Pour into the pie plate.

3. Bake the pie in the preheated oven for about 20–25 minutes or until the edge has set but the center is still very soft. Let cool, remove from the plate, then dust lightly with confectioners' sugar.

4. To make the custard sauce, dissolve the instant espresso powder with 2–3 tablespoons of hot water, then beat into the prepared custard sauce. Slowly add the light cream, beating constantly, then stir in the coffee-flavored liqueur, if desired. Serve slices of the pie in a pool of espresso custard with strawberries.

1

2

4

Frozen Mississippi Mud Pie

INGREDIENTS

Cuts into 6–8 slices

1 quantity ginger crumb crust
  (*see* page 146)
2 cups chocolate ice cream
2 cups coffee-flavored ice cream

For the chocolate topping:

6 oz. chopped semisweet
  dark chocolate
$\frac{1}{4}$ cup light cream
1 tbsp. light corn syrup
1 tsp. vanilla extract
2 oz. white and milk chocolate,
  coarsely grated

HELPFUL HINT

Use the best-quality ice cream that is available for this recipe. Look for chocolate ice cream with added ingredients such as chocolate chips, pieces of toffee, or rippled chocolate. If preferred you can add some raspberries, chopped nuts, or small pieces of chopped white chocolate to both the chocolate and coffee ice cream.

1 Prepare the crumb crust and use to line a 9-inch springform cake pan and then freeze for 30 minutes.

2 Soften the ice cream at room temperature for about 25 minutes. Spoon the chocolate ice cream into the crumb crust, spreading it evenly over the bottom, then spoon the coffee ice cream over the chocolate ice cream, mounding it slightly in the center. Return to the freezer to refreeze the ice cream.

3 For the topping, heat the semisweet dark chocolate with the cream, corn syrup, and vanilla extract in a saucepan. Stir until the chocolate has melted and is smooth. Pour into a bowl and chill in the refrigerator, stirring occasionally, until cold but not set.

4 Spread the cooled chocolate mixture over the top of the frozen pie. Sprinkle with the grated chocolate and return to the freezer for 1½ hours or until firm. Serve at room temperature.

1

2

4

White Chocolate Mousse & Strawberry Tart

INGREDIENTS

Cuts into 10 slices

1 quantity sweet piecrust dough
  (*see* page 140)
¼ cup strawberry jam
1–2 tbsp. kirsch or framboise liqueur
4–6 cups ripe strawberries,
  sliced lengthwise

For the white chocolate mousse:

9 oz. white chocolate, chopped
1½ cups heavy cream
3 tbsp. kirsch or framboise liqueur
1–2 extra-large egg whites (optional)

HELPFUL HINT

This recipe contains raw egg whites, which should be avoided by vulnerable groups including the elderly, young, and pregnant women. If you have concerns, omit from the recipe.

1. Preheat the oven to 400°F. Roll the prepared dough out on a lightly floured surface and use to line a 10-inch cake pan.

2. Line with either foil or nonstick parchment paper and baking beans, then bake blind in the preheated oven for 15–20 minutes. Remove the foil or parchment paper and return to the oven for an additional 5 minutes.

3. To make the mousse, place the white chocolate with 2 tablespoons of water and ½ cup cream in a saucepan and heat gently, stirring until the chocolate has melted and is smooth. Remove from the heat, stir in the kirsch or framboise liqueur, and let cool.

4. Whip the remaining cream until soft peaks form. Fold a spoonful of the cream into the cooled white chocolate mixture, then fold in the remaining cream. If desired, beat the egg whites until stiff and gently fold into the white chocolate cream mixture to make a softer, lighter mousse. Chill in the refrigerator for 15–20 minutes.

5. Heat the strawberry jam with the kirsch or framboise liqueur, and brush or spread half the mixture onto the bottom of the pie shell. Let cool.

6. Spread the chilled chocolate mousse over the jam and arrange the sliced strawberries in concentric circles over the mousse. If necessary, reheat the strawberry jam and glaze the strawberries lightly.

7. Chill the tart in the refrigerator for about 3–4 hours or until the chocolate mousse has set. Cut into slices and serve.

3

4

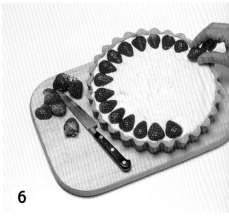

6

Chocolate Raspberry Mille-Feuille

INGREDIENTS

Cuts into 6 slices

1 lb. puff pastry, thawed if frozen
1 quantity chilled Chocolate
   Raspberry Ganache (*see* page 154)
6 cups fresh raspberries, plus extra
   for decorating
confectioners' sugar, for dusting

For the raspberry sauce:

2 cups fresh raspberries
2 tbsp. seedless raspberry jelly
1–2 tbsp. superfine sugar, or to taste
2 tbsp. lemon juice or
   framboise liqueur

HELPFUL HINT

If you prefer, make a single big pastry by leaving the three strips whole in step 2. Slice the finished pastry with a sharp serrated knife.

1 Preheat the oven to 400°F. Lightly grease a large cookie sheet and sprinkle with a little water. Roll out the puff pastry on a lightly floured surface to a rectangle about 11 x 17 inches. Cut into three long strips. Mark each strip crosswise at 2½-inch intervals using a sharp knife; this will make cutting the baked puff pastry easier and neater. Carefully transfer to the cookie sheet, keeping the edges as straight as possible.

2 Bake in the preheated oven for 20 minutes or until well risen and golden brown. Place on a wire rack and let cool. Carefully transfer each rectangle to a work surface, and using a sharp knife, trim the long edges straight. Cut along the knife marks to make 18 rectangles.

3 Place all the ingredients for the raspberry sauce in a food processor and blend until smooth. If the puree is too thick, add a little water. Taste and adjust the sweetness if necessary. Strain into a bowl, cover, and chill in the refrigerator.

4 Place one pastry rectangle on the work surface flat-side down, spread with a little chocolate ganache, and sprinkle with a few fresh raspberries. Spread a second rectangle with a little ganache, place over the first, pressing gently, then sprinkle with a few raspberries. Place a third rectangle on top, flat-side up and spread with a little chocolate ganache.

5 Arrange some raspberries on top and dust lightly with a little confectioners' sugar. Repeat with the remaining pastry rectangles, chocolate ganache, and fresh raspberries.

6 Chill in the refrigerator until needed, and serve with the raspberry sauce and any remaining fresh raspberries.

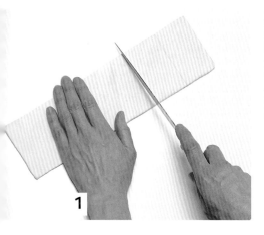

1

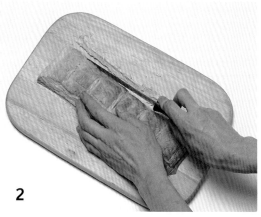

2

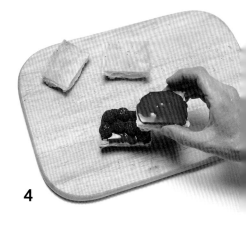

4

Chocolate Brioche Bake

INGREDIENTS

Serves 6

7 oz. semisweet dark chocolate,
   broken into pieces

6 tbsp. unsalted butter

1 large sliced brioche

1 tsp. pure orange oil or 1 tbsp. grated
   orange zest

½ tsp. freshly grated nutmeg

3 large eggs, beaten

2 tbsp. raw sugar

2½ cups milk

unsweetened cocoa and
   confectioners' sugar, for dusting

1   Preheat the oven to 350°F. Lightly grease an ovenproof dish. Melt the chocolate with 2 tablespoons of the butter in a small heatproof bowl set over a saucepan of simmering water. Stir until smooth.

2   Arrange half of the sliced brioche in the ovenproof dish, overlapping the slices slightly, then pour over half of the melted chocolate. Repeat the layers, finishing with a layer of chocolate.

3   Melt the remaining butter in a saucepan. Remove from the heat and stir in the orange oil or zest, the nutmeg, and the beaten eggs. Continuing to stir, add the sugar and finally the milk. Beat thoroughly and pour over the brioche. Let stand for 30 minutes before baking.

4   Bake on the center shelf in the preheated oven for 45 minutes or until the custard is set and the topping is golden brown. Let stand for 5 minutes, then dust with unsweetened cocoa and confectioners' sugar. Serve warm.

HELPFUL HINT

Croissants, fruit buns, or fruit loaves are also suitable for this recipe. It is important that the dish is left to stand for 30 minutes before baking.

2

1

3

Mocha Pie

INGREDIENTS

Cuts into 4–6 slices

1 9-inch ready-made sweet piecrust

For the filling:

4 oz. semisweet dark chocolate,
 broken into pieces
3/4 cup (1 1/2 sticks) unsalted butter
1 cup firmly packed brown sugar
1 tsp. vanilla extract
3 tbsp. strong black coffee

For the topping:

2 cups heavy cream
1/2 cup confectioners' sugar
2 tsp. vanilla extract
1 tsp. instant coffee dissolved in 1
 tsp. boiling water, cooled
grated semisweet dark and white
 chocolate, to decorate

1 Place the prepared pastry shell on a large serving plate and set aside. Melt the chocolate in a heatproof bowl set over a saucepan of simmering water. Ensure the water is not touching the bottom of the bowl. Remove from the heat, stir until smooth, and let cool.

2 Cream the butter, brown sugar, and vanilla extract until light and fluffy, then beat in the cooled chocolate. Add the coffee, pour into the pastry shell, and chill in the refrigerator for about 30 minutes.

3 For the topping, beat the cream until beginning to thicken, then beat in the sugar and vanilla extract. Continue to beat until the cream is softly peaking. Spoon just under half of the cream into a separate bowl and fold in the dissolved coffee.

4 Spread the remaining cream over the filling in the pastry shell. Spoon the coffee-flavored whipped cream evenly over the top, then swirl it decoratively with a metal spatula. Sprinkle with grated chocolate and chill in the refrigerator until ready to serve.

HELPFUL HINT

Using a ready-made pastry shell or pie crust makes this a quickly made pie that looks impressive.

2

3

4

Crunchy Rhubarb Crisp

INGREDIENTS

Serves 6

1 cup all-purpose flour
4 tbsp. butter, softened
²/₃ cup rolled oats
4 tbsp. turbinado sugar
1 tbsp. sesame seeds
¹/₂ tsp. ground cinnamon
1 lb. fresh rhubarb
4 tbsp. superfine sugar, plus extra
   for sprinkling
custard sauce or cream, to serve

TASTY TIP

To make homemade custard, add a few drops vanilla extract to 2¹/₂ cups milk. Pour into a saucepan and bring to a boil. Remove from the heat and let cool. Meanwhile, beat 5 egg yolks and 3 tablespoons superfine sugar together in a mixing bowl until thick and pale in color. Add the milk, stir, and strain into a heavy-based saucepan. Cook on a low heat, stirring constantly until the consistency of heavy cream. Pour over the rhubarb crisp and serve.

1. Preheat the oven to 350°F. Place the flour in a large bowl and cut the butter into cubes. Add to the flour and rub in with your fingertips until the mixture looks like fine bread crumbs, or blend for a few seconds in a food processor

2. Stir in the rolled oats, turbinado sugar, sesame seeds, and cinnamon. Mix well and set aside.

3. Prepare the rhubarb by removing the thick ends of the stems and cut diagonally into 1-inch chunks. Wash thoroughly under cold running water and pat dry with a clean dishtowel. Place the rhubarb in a 1-quart casserole dish.

4. Sprinkle the superfine sugar over the rhubarb and top with the crisp mixture. Level the top of the crisp so that all the fruit is well covered, and press down firmly. If desired, sprinkle a little extra sugar on the top.

5. Place on a cookie sheet and bake in the preheated oven for 40–50 minutes or until the fruit is soft and the topping is golden brown. Sprinkle the pudding with some more sugar and serve hot with custard sauce or cream.

2

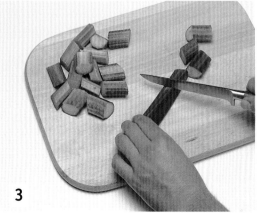

3

4

Chocolate Crepes

INGREDIENTS

Makes approx. 8

For the crepes:
3/4 cup all-purpose flour
1 tbsp. unsweetened cocoa
1 tsp. superfine sugar
1/2 tsp. freshly grated nutmeg
2 large eggs
3/4 cup milk
6 tbsp. unsalted butter, melted

For the mango sauce:
1 ripe peeled and diced mango
1/4 cup white wine
2 tbsp. superfine sugar
2 tbsp. rum

For the filling:
8 oz. semisweet dark chocolate
1/3 cup heavy cream
3 eggs, separated
2 tbsp. superfine sugar

1. Preheat the oven to 400°F. To make the crepes, sift the flour, unsweetened cocoa, sugar, and nutmeg into a bowl, and make a well in the center. Beat the eggs and milk together, then gradually beat into the flour mixture to form a batter. Stir in 1/4 cup of the melted butter and let stand for 1 hour.

2. Heat a 7-inch nonstick skillet and brush with a little melted butter. Add about 3 tablespoons of the batter and swirl to cover the bottom of the skillet. Cook over a medium heat for 1–2 minutes, flip over, and cook for an additional 40 seconds. Repeat with the remaining batter. Stack the crepes interleaving with wax paper.

3. To make the sauce, place the mango, white wine, and sugar in a saucepan, and bring to a boil over a medium heat, then simmer for 2–3 minutes, stirring constantly. When the mixture has thickened, add the rum. Chill in the refrigerator.

4. For the filling, melt the chocolate and cream in a small, heavy saucepan over a medium heat. Stir until smooth, then let cool. Beat the egg yolks with the sugar for 3–5 minutes or until the mixture is pale and creamy, then beat in the chocolate mixture.

5. Beat the egg whites until stiff, then add a little to the chocolate mixture. Stir in the remainder. Spoon a little of the mixture onto a crepe. Fold in half, then fold in half again, forming a triangle. Repeat with the remaining crepes.

6. Brush the crepes with a little melted butter and bake in the preheated oven for 15–20 minutes or until the filling is set. Serve hot or cold with the mango sauce.

1

2

5

Iced Bakewell Tart

INGREDIENTS

Cuts into 10 slices

For the rich pastry:

1½ cups all-purpose flour

pinch of salt

5 tbsp. butter, cut into small pieces

4 tbsp. shortening, cut into small pieces

2 medium egg yolks, beaten

For the filling:

½ cup (1 stick) butter, melted

½ cup superfine sugar

1 cup ground almonds

2 extra-large eggs, beaten

few drops almond extract

2 tbsp. seedless raspberry jelly

For the icing:

1 cup confectioners' sugar, sifted

6–8 tsp. fresh lemon juice

¼ cup toasted, slivered almonds

1 Preheat the oven to 400°F. Place the flour and salt in a bowl, and rub in the butter and shortening until the mixture resembles bread crumbs. Alternatively, blend quickly, in short bursts, in a food processor.

2 Add the eggs with enough water to make a soft, pliable dough. Knead lightly on a floured board, then chill in the refrigerator for about 30 minutes. Roll out the pastry and use to line a 9-inch, loose-bottomed tart pan.

3 For the filling, mix together the melted butter, sugar, almonds, and beaten eggs, and add a few drops of almond extract. Spread the base of the pastry shell with the raspberry jelly and spoon over the egg mixture.

4 Bake in the preheated oven for about 30 minutes or until the filling is firm and golden brown. Remove from the oven and let cool completely.

5 When the tart is cold, make the frosting by mixing together the confectioners' sugar and lemon juice, a little at a time, until the frosting is smooth and of a spreadable consistency.

6 Spread the frosting over the tart, leave to set for 2–3 minutes, and sprinkle with the almonds. Chill in the refrigerator for about 10 minutes, and serve.

TASTY TIP

It is not essential to use raspberry jelly. Use any seedless jelly available. Blackberry jelly would work particularly well.

2

3

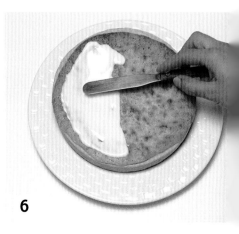

6

Apricot & Almond Slice

INGREDIENTS

Cuts into 10 slices

2 tbsp. turbinado sugar

¼ cup slivered almonds

14 oz. canned drained apricot halves

1 cup (2 sticks) butter

1 cup superfine sugar

4 large eggs

1½ cups plus 3 tbsp
self-rising flour

¼ cup ground almonds

½ tsp. almond extract

⅓ cup dried apricots, chopped

3 tbsp. honey

3 tbsp. coarsely chopped
almonds, toasted

HELPFUL HINT

This cake should keep for about 3 to 5 days if stored correctly. Let the cake cool completely, then remove from the pan and discard the lining paper. Store in an airtight container lined with wax paper or parchment paper, and keep in a cool place.

1 Preheat the oven to 350°F. Grease an 8-inch square pan and line with nonstick parchment paper.

2 Sprinkle the turbinado sugar and the slivered almonds over the parchment paper, then arrange the apricot halves cut-side down on top.

3 Cream butter and sugar together in a large bowl until light and fluffy.

4 Gradually beat the eggs into the butter mixture, adding a spoonful of flour after each addition of egg.

5 When all the eggs have been added, stir in the remaining flour and ground almonds, and mix thoroughly.

6 Add the almond extract and the apricots, and stir well.

7 Spoon the mixture into the prepared pan, taking care not to dislodge the apricot halves. Bake in the preheated oven for 1 hour or until golden and firm to touch.

8 Remove from the oven and let cool slightly for 15–20 minutes. Turn out carefully, discard the parchment paper, and transfer to a serving dish. Pour the honey over the top of the cake, sprinkle with the toasted almonds, and serve.

2

5

8

Strawberry Flan

INGREDIENTS

Cuts into 6 slices

Sweet pastry:

1½ cups all-purpose flour
4 tbsp. butter
4 tbsp. shortening
2 tsp. superfine sugar
1 large egg yolk, beaten

For the filling:

1 large egg, plus 1 extra egg yolk
4 tbsp. superfine sugar
3 tbsp. all-purpose flour
2½ cups milk
few drops vanilla extract
3 cups cleaned and hulled
  strawberries
mint leaves, to decorate

TASTY TIP

In the summer, why not try topping the flan with a variety of mixed fruits? If liked, heat 3 tablespoons seedless raspberry jelly with 2 teaspoons lemon juice. Stir until smooth, then use to brush over the fruit. Let set before serving.

1 Preheat the oven to 400°F. Place the flour, butter, and shortening in a food processor and blend until the mixture resembles fine bread crumbs. Stir in the sugar, then, with the machine running, add the egg yolk and enough water to make a stiff dough. Knead lightly, cover, and chill in the refrigerator for 30 minutes.

2 Roll out the pastry and use to line a 9-inch, loose-bottomed tart pan. Place a piece of wax paper in the pastry shell, and cover with baking beans. Bake in the preheated oven for 15–20 minutes until just firm. Set aside until cool.

3 Make the filling by beating the eggs and sugar together until thick and pale. Gradually stir in the flour and then the milk. Pour into a small saucepan, and simmer for 3–4 minutes, stirring throughout.

4 Add the vanilla extract to taste, then pour into a bowl and let cool. Cover with wax paper to prevent a skin from forming.

5 When the filling is cold, beat until smooth, then pour onto the cooked flan shell. Slice the strawberries and arrange on the top of the filling. Decorate with the mint leaves and serve.

2

3

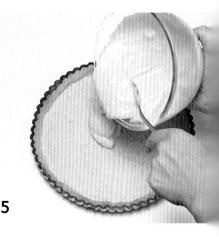

5

Rich Double-Crust Plum Pie

INGREDIENTS

Serves 6

For the pastry:
6 tbsp. butter
6 tbsp. shortening
2 cups all-purpose flour
2 large egg yolks

For the filling:
1 lb. fresh plums
4 tbsp. superfine sugar
1 tbsp. milk
a little extra superfine sugar

1 Preheat the oven to 400°F. Make the pastry by rubbing the butter and shortening into the flour until it resembles fine bread crumbs, or blend in a food processor. Add the egg yolks and enough water to make a soft dough. Knead lightly, then wrap, and leave in the refrigerator for about 30 minutes.

2 Meanwhile, prepare the fruit. Rinse and dry the plums, then cut in half and remove the pits. Slice the plums into chunks, and cook in a saucepan with 2 tablespoons of the sugar and 2 tablespoons of water for 5–7 minutes or until slightly softened. Remove from the heat and add the remaining sugar to taste and let cool.

3 Roll out half the chilled dough on a lightly floured surface and use to line the base and sides of a 1-quart casserole dish. Let the dough hang over the edge of the dish. Spoon in the prepared plums.

4 Roll out the remaining dough to use as the lid, and brush the edge with some water. Wrap the dough around the rolling pin and place over the plums.

5 Press the edges together to seal, and mark a decorative edge around the rim of the pastry by pinching with the thumb and forefinger or using the back of a fork.

6 Brush the lid with milk, and make a few slits in the top. Use any trimmings to decorate the top. Place on a cookie sheet and bake in the preheated oven for 30 minutes or until golden. Sprinkle with a little superfine sugar and serve hot or cold.

HELPFUL HINT
Fresh plums are available from May to late October. When choosing plums, look for ones that are firm and give slightly to pressure. Avoid those with cracks, soft spots, or brown discolorations.

2

4

5

Baked Apple Dumplings

INGREDIENTS

Makes 4

2 cups self-rising flour
$\frac{1}{4}$ tsp. salt
$\frac{1}{2}$ cup shredded suet
4 medium apples
4–6 tsp. mincemeat
1 large egg white, beaten
2 tsp. superfine sugar
custard or vanilla sauce, to serve

TASTY TIP

To make vanilla sauce, blend $1\frac{1}{2}$ tablespoons cornstarch with 3 tablespoons milk to a smooth paste. Bring a little less than $1\frac{1}{4}$ cups milk to just below boiling point. Stir in the cornstarch paste and cook over a gentle heat, stirring throughout until thick and smooth. Remove from the heat and add 1 tablespoon superfine sugar, a pat of butter, and $\frac{1}{2}$ teaspoon vanilla extract. Stir until the sugar and butter have melted, then serve.

1. Preheat the oven to 400°F. Lightly grease a baking pan. Place the flour and salt in a large bowl and stir in the suet.

2. Add just enough water to the mixture to make a soft, but not sticky, dough, using your fingertips.

3. Turn dough onto a lightly floured board and knead lightly into a ball.

4. Divide the dough into four pieces and roll out each piece into a thin square, large enough to encase the apples.

5. Peel and core the apples and place 1 apple in the center of each square of pastry.

6. Fill center of the apple with mincemeat, brush the edges of each pastry square with water, and draw the corners up to meet over each apple.

7. Press the edges of the pastry firmly together, and decorate with pastry leaves and shapes made from the extra pastry trimmings.

8. Place the apples on the prepared baking pan, brush with the egg white, and sprinkle with the sugar.

9. Bake in the preheated oven for 30 minutes or until golden and the pastry and apples are cooked. Serve the apple dumplings hot with the custard or vanilla sauce.

2

6

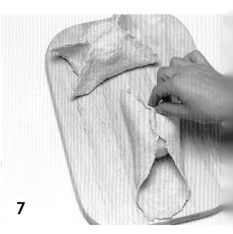

7

Jam Roly-Poly

INGREDIENTS

Serves 6

2 cups self-rising flour
$^1/_4$ tsp. salt
$^1/_2$ cup shredded suet
$^2/_3$ cup water
3 tbsp. strawberry jam
1 tbsp. milk, to glaze
1 tsp. superfine sugar
fruit sauce, to serve

TASTY TIP

To make fruit sauce, warm 4 tablespoons jam, for example, raspberry jam, with $^1/_4$ cup water or orange juice. Stir until smooth. Blend 2 teaspoons arrowroot with 1 tablespoon water or juice to a smooth paste. Bring the mixture to almost boiling, then stir in the blended arrowroot. Cook, stirring, until the mixture thickens slightly and clears, then serve with Jam Roly-Poly.

1. Preheat the oven to 400°F. Make the pastry by sifting the flour and salt into a large bowl.

2. Add the suet and mix lightly, then add the water, a little at a time, and mix to form a soft and pliable dough. Take care not to make the dough too wet.

3. Turn the dough out onto a lightly floured board and knead gently until smooth.

4. Roll the dough out into a 9 x 11-inch rectangle.

5. Spread the jam over the pastry, leaving a border of $^1/_2$ inch all around. Fold the border over the jam and brush the edges with water.

6. Lightly roll up the rectangle from one of the short sides, seal the top edge, and press the ends together. Do not roll pudding up too tightly.

7. Turn the pudding upside-down onto a large piece of wax paper large enough to come halfway up the sides. If using nonstick paper, then grease lightly.

8. Fasten the ends of the paper to make a boat-shaped paper case for the pudding to sit in, and to leave room for the roly-poly to expand.

9. Brush the pudding lightly with milk and sprinkle with the sugar. Bake in the preheated oven for 30–40 minutes or until well risen and golden. Serve immediately with the fruit sauce.

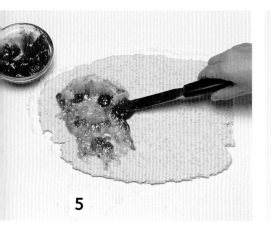

5

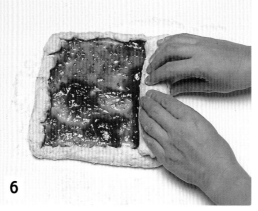

6

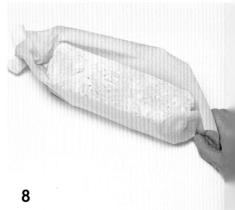

8

Egg Custard Tart

INGREDIENTS

Cuts into 6 slices

Sweet pastry:
4 tbsp. butter
4 tbsp. shortening
1 cups all-purpose flour
1 large egg yolk, beaten
2 tsp. superfine sugar

For the filling:
1¼ cups milk
2 large eggs, plus
 1 large egg yolk
2 tbsp. superfine sugar
½ tsp. freshly grated nutmeg

HELPFUL HINT
Eggs should always be stored in the refrigerator—keep them in the box they came in. One way to test if an egg is fresh is to place an uncooked egg in a bowl of water— if it lies at the bottom, it is fresh; if it tilts, it is older (use for frying or scrambling); if it floats, discard.

1 Preheat the oven to 400°F. Grease an 8-inch flan ring.

2 Make the pastry by cutting the butter and shortening into small cubes. Add to the flour in a large bowl and rub in until the mixture resembles fine bread crumbs.

3 Add the egg, sugar, and enough water to form a soft and pliable dough. Turn onto a lightly floured board and knead. Wrap and chill in the refrigerator for 30 minutes.

4 Roll the pastry out onto a lightly floured surface or pastry board, and use to line the greased flan ring. Place in the refrigerator.

5 Warm the milk in a small saucepan. Beat together the eggs, egg yolk, and sugar.

6 Pour the milk into the egg mixture and beat until well blended.

7 Strain through a sieve into the pastry shell. Place the flan ring on a cookie sheet.

8 Sprinkle the top of the tart with nutmeg, and bake in the preheated oven for about 15 minutes.

9 Turn the oven down to 325°F and bake for an additional 30 minutes or until the custard has set. Serve hot or cold.

2

5

7

Index